Mississippi

Bob Dylan's
midlife masterpiece

Jochen Markhorst

To Marga

Stick with me baby, stick with me anyhow
Things should start to get interestin' right about now

CONTENTS

"We had that on the *Time Out of Mind* album. It wasn't recorded very well but, thank God, it never got out, so we recorded it again."

(Dylan on *Mississippi*, press conference Rome, 2001)

I   Sexy Afro-polyrhythm

Things got contentious once in the parking lot. He tried to convince me that the song had to be *"sexy, sexy and more sexy."* I know about sexy, too. He reminded me of Sam Phillips, who had once said the same thing to John Prine about a song, but the circumstances were not similar.

(David Fricke interview for *Rolling Stone,* 2001)

The *A&E Series Biography*, Peter Guralnick's brilliant documentary about Sam Phillips is broadcast in 2000: "Sam Phillips - The Man Who Invented Rock 'n' Roll". The film lasts 90 fascinating minutes, and towards the end the sons of Phillips, Jerry and Knox, talk about their father's interference with John Prine.

At the beginning of 1979 John Prine records a particularly atypical record, *Pink Cadillac*. After five albums full of widely admired songs, songs for which even Dylan takes off his hat, Prine wants to profess his love for good old rock 'n' roll with his sixth album. For the first and only time in his career, the lyrics are of minor importance. It had to be *good, honest music*, according to Prine in the liner notes of the album.

More poetically he repeats it in the liner notes of the unsurpassed compilation album *Great Days*, also written down by David Fricke in 1993:

> I wanted to do something noisy, something like if you had a buddy with a band and you walked into his house and you could hear 'em practicing in the basement.

He would like to record that album in the studio of the legendary Sun Records producer Sam Phillips in Memphis, led by sons Jerry and Knox Phillips, who will also produce Prine's record. However, to Prine's delight, one day Dad stops by - and he takes charge of the production right away.

Today "Saigon" and "How Lucky" are on the roll.

The old Phillips only came in to say hello, hears Prine's - in his ears – "awful" singing and just *has* to do something. First he thunders his displeasure with Prine's limp vocals into the studio via the intercom from the control room. "And then he put extra reverb, the slap-back echo, on his voice," Prine tells. "You felt like Moses talking to the burning bush."

When it still doesn't suffice, Phillips slides on his kitchen chair into Prine's comfort zone and snaps, millimeters from Prine's face, eyes maniacally wide open and bulging: "*And John, can you put some sex in it?*"

In the documentary, son Knox, who does look a lot like his father, imitates it in a terrifying way, including the wildly insane look.

The next recording of "Saigon" satisfies Sam, but some question marks may be placed over his judgement - Prine's vocals on this final recording actually do sound rather twisted, unnatural and not very spontaneous. The protagonist nevertheless looks back with pride and affection, in the same documentary. "I was in the studio with Sam Phillips, you know. If Sam told me to stand on my head and sing that night, I would've."

Phillips wanting to hear sex in "Saigon" is conceivable, indeed:

> You got everything that a girl should grow
> I'm so afraid to kiss you I might lose control
> You can hold me tighter but turn loose of my gun
> It's a sentimental present all the way from Saigon

But why Daniel Lanois thinks "Mississippi" should sound *"sexy, sexy and more sexy"* is less understandable. Dylan does have a point when he says, "The circumstances were not similar."

However, Dylan's next statement, still in the same paragraph of that interview with David Fricke for *Rolling Stone*, is once again familiarly enigmatic:

> I tried to explain that the song had more to do with the Declaration of Independence, the Constitution and the Bill of Rights than witch doctors, and just couldn't be thought of as some kind of ideological voodoo thing.

My my. The Declaration of Independence, the Constitution and the Bill of Rights, and before that Dylan also points to a *hidden expressive meaning behind the lyrics*.

Poor Daniel Lanois; that indeed does require some explanation. The ease with which Dylan shifts complete verses back and forth and the untroubled way with which he deletes entire verse lines (for example, the third outtake opens with *I'm standing in the shadows with an aching heart / I'm looking at the world tear itself apart*) doesn't really support the statement that Dylan himself sees very clearly what he wants to express in the text.

Even more puzzling is Dylan's analysis a little earlier in the interview:

> Lanois didn't see it. Thought it was pedestrian. Took it down the Afro-polyrhythm route — multirhythm drumming, that sort of thing. Polyrhythm has its place, but it doesn't work for knifelike lyrics trying to convey majesty and heroism.

"Multi-rhythm drumming" and "Afro-polyrhythm" does sound a bit hysterical, frankly. On the rejected, breathtakingly beautiful recordings, the three versions which will eventually be released on *The Bootleg Series Vol. 8: Tell Tale Signs: Rare and Unreleased 1989-2006* (2008), there is no such thing. Lanois creates a J.J. Cale-like atmosphere, including a tapping foot – it really is not *that* fancy. It almost seems as if Dylan confuses the song with the also rejected recordings of "Series Of Dreams", a song that - although it cannot be catalogued under the heading "*majesty and heroism*" - is indeed filled with a cascade of furious, overwhelming drumming, with "multi-rhythm drumming" and "Afro-polyrhythm".

Sexy it *is*, though.

II   Lomax' death

Only one thing I did wrong
Stayed in Mississippi a day too long

 John Lomax, the groundbreaking musicologist and folklorist to whom we owe the survival of hundreds of folk songs and Lead Belly's career, dies on January 26, 1948 during a visit to his native state of Mississippi, in Greenville. He is there as guest of honour on *John Lomax Day*, organized by the mayor, celebrating Lomax' eightieth birthday. According to legend, John sings the song "Big-Leg Rose" shortly after his arrival, during the press conference, and suffers his fatal heart attack after the last line:

The only thing I ever done wrong
Stayed in Mississippi one day too long

At least, that's what it says in Greg Milner's *Perfecting Sound Forever: The Story of Recorded Music* (2009), and other sources report as well that these last words of "Big-Leg Rose" are also the last words of the legendary music pioneer.

It's, like most stories about celebrities' last words, a little too good to be true. In the Library Of Congress one can indeed find Lomax' 1939 recording of "Big-Leg Rosie" (with *ie*). Sung by a group of prisoners of the infamous Parchman Penitentary in Mississippi on May 24th, who accompany themselves with ax-cutting; "performed by Frank 'Gulfport Red' Mixon and unidentified performers (vocals with ax-cutting) at State Penitentiary, Camp #1".

In his last book, the autobiography *Adventures Of A Ballad Hunter* (1947), Lomax does remember that spring night in Mississippi:

> The singers on the ground in front, with hoes and axes and a log pile, staged work-gang songs. That night Alan and I heard for the first time "Big Leg Rosie," "Stewball," "Po' Lazus," the "Bad Man Ballad," "Diamond Joe," and many another. Our machine was not handling the aluminum disks without considerable scratching and sputtering, but we captured the tunes accurately enough to be transcribed.

The recording, which can be listened to via the website of the Library Of Congress, is indeed quite damaged here and there, but is clear enough to hear that there is no singing about *"Mississippi"* and no *"day too long"*.

But the song titles Lomax lists here offer plenty of other aha-moments:

This "Po' Lazarus" (John Lomax writes it as *Po' Lazus*) is the primal version of the recording that will later be used in the Coen Brothers film *O Brother Where Art Thou* (2000) and thus gets a surprising tail end for the cantor, James Carter. Mainly thanks to son Alan Lomax. Because the handy tape recorder was invented, with which recordings of much better quality can be made, Alan Lomax returns to Parchman Penitentary in 1959 to re-record as many songs as possible twenty years after his father - including "Po' Lazarus".

This version, which is in the name of "James Carter & the Prisoners", is on the soundtrack of the film. The soundtrack is a huge hit. John Lomax' granddaughter Anna, the manager of the Alan Lomax Archive, and producer T-Bone Burnett make every effort to find James Carter, who indeed turns out to be alive, who can't remember a thing from the recording forty years ago and who to his surprise is allowed to accept a check for $20,000. *Really* stunned, however, he is upon learning that the album sells better than the latest CD's of Mariah Carey and Michael Jackson. Once he's processed that, he expresses his desire to reassure The Prince of Pop: "You tell Michael that I'll slow down so that he can catch up with me."

In the summer of 1967 Dylan sings "Po' Lazarus" in the Basement, of which unfortunately only one minute has been preserved (on CD 1 of *The Basement Tapes Complete*). Echoes of the song can be heard a few years later in Dylan's prison song "George Jackson"; the "Lord Lord" refrain line is a copy of the "Lawd Lawd" refrain line from "Po' Lazarus".

Dylan sings "Diamond Joe" on *Good As I Been To You*, which, by the way, is not the same "Diamond Joe" he sings in his movie *Masked and Anonymous*.

"Stewball", the template for Lennon's "Happy Xmas (War Is Over)", is on the repertoire of Pete Seeger, The Greenbriar Boys, Woody Guthrie, Joan Baez and Peter, Paul & Mary, to name but a few of Dylan's most direct influences, and "Bad Man Ballad" is one of many variants of "Little Sadie", which Dylan will record for *Self Portrait*.

In short: all songs that end up in Dylan's luggage. A line from "Big Leg Rosie", the song in this same row, to Dylan should be obvious. But there isn't one. The quoted verse line, the supposed last words of Lomax, *"The only thing I ever done wrong / Stayed in Mississippi one day too long"*, do not origin from "Big Leg Rosie" but from "Rosie" - the same maiden name, indeed, but a different melody, a different lyrics, a different song:

> *Little Rosie, your hair grow long,*
> *'Cause I'm goin' to see your daddy when I get home.*
> ***They ain't but the one thing that I done wrong.***
> ***I stayed in Mississippi just one day too long.***
> *Come and get me an'-a take me home,*
> *These lifetime devils, they won't leave me lone.*
> *Well, I come here wid a hundred years,*
> *A tree fall on me, I don't bit mo' care.*

John Lomax' son Alan, remembers it in Chapter 7 of his *Selected Writings*, the chapter "Reels And Work Songs":

For the last song in this group of records, we come to the most intense, the angriest, the most passionate of the work songs in the South. Strangely enough, it is called "Rosie." "Rosie" is sung full-throated by fifty men, flatweeding in an irrigation ditch in Mississippi. The hoes flash up together and all splash green.

Not a word about his father's death in this excerpt. He was there when John Lomax had that fatal heart attack, so it's rather unlikely he would leave that out of the discussion of "Rosie". If it had been true.

Alan then, while his father still is in the hospital in a coma from which he won't wake up again, is standing in and represents his father at the inauguration the next day.

He stays an extra day in Mississippi.

III Belshazzar on the steppe

Every step of the way we walk the line
Your days are numbered, so are mine
Time is pilin' up, we struggle and we scrape
We're all boxed in, nowhere to escape

 In 1820 Heinrich Heine writes his ballad "Belsazar", about the last evening of the Babylonian king. That evening, probably October 12, 539 BC, Belshazzar organizes a party. During the feast he is so audacious as to call for the "sacred goblets", goblets that his grandfather Nebuchadnezzar had stolen from the Temple of Jerusalem during the destruction. He fills a sacred goblet with wine, rises, gulps it in one go to the bottom and, to the great delight of the partygoers present, roars insulting texts about this so-called "Jehovah", that God of the Jews (*Jehovah! I proclaim to you my eternal scorn, for I am the King of Babylon!*).

Which he shouldn't have done.

A hand appears out of nowhere. The hand floats through the room and writes "letters of fire" on the wall. The frenzied revelry is extinguished in one blow and with knocking knees the pale Belshazzar stares at the incomprehensible signs on the wall. The magicians are called in, but no one can decipher those strange symbols.

Belshazzar, however, was murdered that same night by his bodyguard.

Heine re-tells the story from Daniel 5, leaving out, to increase the suspense, the punch line; in the Bible story, the Jewish slave Daniel is brought in, who can indeed tell what those writings on the wall mean: *mene mene tekel ufarsin* – "numbered, numbered, weighed and divided". By what God means to say, Daniel helpfully explains to Belsazar, that your days are numbered, that you have been found to be too light, and that your kingdom will be divided.

Like "writings on the wall", "your days are numbered" has become an expression from which the biblical origins have evaporated; they have both become so common that no one thinks of the Old Testament, Daniel or that cheeky Belshazzar anymore.

Neither does the esteemed Dylan researcher from Albuquerque, Scott Warmuth point to the Bible, but rather to Henry Rollins. Not entirely unjustified; "Mississippi" has indeed borrowed some four, five fragments and word combinations from Rollins' poems and prose but attributing this "your days are numbered" to Rollins' influence is a bit too much credit.

The expression has existed for more than twenty centuries (the Book of Daniel was probably written around 165 B.C.) and Dylan himself has used it way before Rollins did (in "When The Ship Comes In", 1963).

There, in the furious "When The Ship Comes In", the lieder poet uses the expression in the old, biblical sense: it announces the imminent, ruthless destruction of the enemy and introduces further biblical metaphors ("Pharaoh's Tribe" and "Goliath").

However, the protagonist in "Mississippi" is, just like the poet, a couple of decades older and therefore calmer - in this first quatrain, it is one of the seven expressions the narrator chooses to express something like fatigue, hopelessness, existential loneliness.

Individually, the seven expressions are not that spectacular. "Every step of the way" is an ordinary, commonplace phrase, just like "we walk the line" has been established since long before Johnny Cash. The expression has been documented since 1874, indicating the line along which the prisoners in Port Arthur, Tasmania, had to walk during the convict exercise hour, but Johnny Cash probably picked it up from Merle Haggard's "Sixteen Tons" (1947):

> I was born one mornin', it was drizzlin' rain
> Fightin' and trouble are my middle name
> I was raised in the canebrake by an ol' mama lion
> Can't no-a high-toned woman make me walk the line

Cash uses it in the same sense as Merle Haggard: "staying true to your wife" - *I find it very easy to be true... because you're mine, I walk the line.* And the songwriter Dylan also uses it often enough with that content ("Can't Wait", "Shelter From The Storm", "Up To Me", "Let's Keep It Between Us"), but in "Mississippi" the meaning shifts.

In "Mississippi" the poet is looking for synonyms. In general, Dylan does not shy away from *repetitio*, from literal repetitions of the same word or an identical word combination. "Everything's Broken", "Wiggle Wiggle", "Hard Rain", "Rainy Day Women"... at every stage of his career the bard writes "list songs", songs that rely on the power of repetitio. But here he chooses the *accumulatio*, the enumeration of equivalents, all of which in this case have a rather Lutheran message: life is suffering.

Characteristic for Dylan's later work is his multi-coloured palette. The seven equivalents are in themselves, separately, not very adventurous. But the special power of this opening coup is the accumulation of expressions from all corners of Dylan's cultural baggage.

The Bible and Johnny Cash are followed by *struggle and scrape*, which echoes Elvis' gospel records, or to be more precise: "If We Never Meet Again" that Elvis sings together with The Jordanaires on his first gospel record *His Hand In Mine* (1960) ("As we struggle through this life and strife"). And "boxed in", the unusual equivalent of *nowhere to escape*, with which the quatrain closes, indirectly penetrates Dylan's vocabulary via those old Lomax recordings, via "Bad Man Ballad", but Dylan undoubtedly is more familiar with Cisco

Houston's adaptation thereof ("Badman's Blunder") and the hit the Kingston Trio scored with it in 1960:

He was steppin' right along (I was hot-footin' it)
But he was steppin' too slow (It was a hot day)
Got surrounded by a sheriff (Boxed in)
In Mexico (I didn't even have a chance to see the country)

Only the origin of the preceding, tautological *nowhere to escape*, seems to be a bit further from Dylan's cradle - in the American Songbook, in the Bible or at Elvis it is not to be found, in any case. Journalists do use it, usually to dramatize coverage of a fire catastrophe ("Power suddenly went out throughout the eight-story building. There was nowhere to escape. The staircases led down into the fire", *New York Times*, December 7, 2012).

Though with the receptive lyricist Dylan, the source is more literary, perhaps. Chekhov, then. Dylan repeatedly expresses his admiration for the great Russian writer, even suggests in *Chronicles* that *Blood On The Tracks* is based on short stories by Chekhov, building on the 1978 *Playboy* interview: "Chekhov is my favourite writer."

Traces can be found throughout Dylan's entire oeuvre, true. The fascination for *trains*, anyway, the light-absurd, pointless dialogues ("Clothes Line Saga" could have easily been written by the Russian), "Up To Me", "God Knows" (Chekhov's most-used stop word), "Seven Days"... all songs in which remarkable twists, idiom and set descriptions seem to come from Chekhov.

And anyway, the entire song "Mississippi" breathes a Chekhov-like, Russian melancholy, and that unusual word combination *nowhere to escape* can indeed be found with the Russian as well. In his magnificent youth work "The Steppe", the novella with which he more or less breaks through, in 1888:

> On a hot day when there is nowhere to escape from the sultry, stifling heat, the splash of water and the loud breathing of a man bathing sounds like good music to the ear.

The novella is a semi-autobiographical account of a journey to Chekhov's native region, the Mississippi of Russia, the district of Rostov in southern Russia, at the Sea of Azov and the mouth of the Don. Perhaps the most Dylanesque is the lesson that the youthful protagonist learns from his older companions: "Русский человек любит вспоминать, но не любит жить ("Russkij chelovek ljubit vspominat', no ne ljubit zhit"):

A Russian man loves reminiscing, but he does not love living.

Chekhov is talking about the narrator of "Mississippi".

IV   Bertolt, Bobby, Blind & Boy

City's just a jungle; more games to play
Trapped in the heart of it, tryin' to get away
I was raised in the country, I been workin' in the town
I been in trouble ever since I set my suitcase down

Bertolt Brecht is quite proud of himself. On September 4, 1921, he writes in his diary about his "groundbreaking discovery",

> *that actually no one has ever described the big city as a jungle. Where are their heroes, their colonizers, their victims? The hostility of the great city, its malicious stone consistency, its Babylonian confusion of languages, in short: its poetry is not yet created.*

 In the same weeks, Brecht writes *Im Dickicht der Städte* ("In the Jungle of Cities"), a dizzying piece in which Brecht is not too concerned about a logical plot or understandable motives but rather shows different stages of a catastrophic quarrel between two men. With a vague, homoerotic undertone, so some like to see a dramatic portrayal of a *Rimbaud-and-Verlaine*-like relationship, but the main theme is: loneliness - extra sharp-edged because the men, despite being in the big, busy city of Chicago, are actually mostly lonely. Most disconsolate expressed by the timber merchant Shlink: "The infinite loneliness of man makes enmity an unattainable goal."

By the way, Brecht's complacent diary entry is yet another fine example of the great playwright's *Love & Theft* - earlier in his diaries he explains his admiration for Upton Sinclair's *The Jungle* (1905), the social-realist novel that compares the city - not coincidentally also Chicago - to a jungle.

When Dylan writes "Mississippi", *jungle* as a metaphor for "big city" is long established. Not only in books, newspapers and films, but also in songs. Songs that are in Dylan's record cabinet as well, anyway. Bobby Darin, for instance.

The 1968 album *Born Walden Robert Cassotto* marks a rather radical career break for Bobby Darin ("He changed his name when he saw a sign outside a Chinese restaurant that said *Mandarin Duck* – the first three letters were burned out," as radiomaker Dylan reveals in his *Theme Time Radio Hour,* episode 8, "Coffee"). He leaves his record label, writes all the songs himself and converts to folk rock, sociocritical lyrics and an unpolished singing style, much more unpolished than the crooning style which made him great. One of the songs, "Long Line Rider", even causes some controversy, which gets him attention from folk magazine *Broadside.*

In the 1969 March/April issue Dylan's old comrades and doormats print an article from the *New York Post* of February 1: "Censored Darin Sings a Song of Protest". The controversy is painfully petty by today's standards. In the song Darin expresses his amazement at an alleged cover-up operation after the discovery of some unidentified skeletons on a prison site. Remarkably smooth investigation concludes that the corpses were buried there before there was any prison at all, and Darin raises suggestive questions:

{}

All the records show so clear
Not a single man was here
Anyway
That's the tale the warden tells
As he counts his empty shells
By the day
Hey, long line rider, turn away.

Just before a television performance (The Jackie Gleason Show, January '69) record company CBS sends a telegram with the order to delete the above words. Enraged Darin walks out, a scandal seems unavoidable, but it doesn't really get off the ground.

The song and the story behind it have long since been forgotten, but the flop album itself stands the test of time; it's a beautiful album with beautiful songs ("I Can See The Wind", especially, the Leonard Cohen rip-off "In Memoriam" and the Moby Grape-like "Change"). However, style, change of course and the level of protest are not the only indications that Darin is trying to level his idol Dylan. He's already recorded some successful Dylan covers, will record even more beautiful ones in the coming years (his "I'll Be Your Baby Tonight" is one of the most successful covers of that evergreen), and on this record Dylan's influence is evident from the lyrics Darin writes:

We live in a jingle jangle jungle
You're only worth what you can buy
So keep on workin' hard
To keep your own back yard
Teach your kids that God
Ain't fiction
Contradiction
In this jingle jangle jungle you call home.

Dylan undoubtedly knows the record and the song, but *jungle* as a metaphor for the big city is more likely to have come to him through Phil Ochs' "Lou Marsh" (or Pete Seeger's version thereof):

> *Now the streets are empty, now the streets are dark*
> *So keep an eye on shadows and never pass the park*
> *For the city is a jungle when the law is out of sight*
> *Death lurks in El Barrio with the orphans of the night*

"The city is a jungle when the law is out of sight"... the image plus the words that match the opening of Dylan's "Mississippi", the opening verses that poetically introduce the oppression, hopelessness and anguish of the protagonist.

After the sixth verse, the *accumulatio*, the accumulation of the equivalents all expressing approximately the same claustrophobic, Kafkaesque distress, seems to come to an end, and the plot can unfold:

> *I was raised in the country, I been workin' in the town*
> *I been in trouble ever since I set my suitcase down*

... promising a novel-like plot. The trouble, the drastic event in the main character's life is coming up. A first character description is also given: boy from the countryside, who has to make a living in the metropolitan jungle - and it don't come easy, as evidenced by the beautiful, lyrical suitcase line.

It's one of the most beautiful lines in the song, a line with the shine of a polished, old-fashioned blues cliché, but actually a Dylan original - at best it does echo a hint of Blind Lemon Jefferson, "Easy Rider Blues":

I went to the depot
I mean I went to the depot, set my suitcase down
The blues overtake me and the tears come rollin' down

Blind Lemon is a common thread in Dylan's oeuvre. "See That My Grave Is Kept Clean" on the first record, which pops up again in the Basement as "One Kind Favor", "High Water Blues" as template for "Down In The Flood", Blind Lemon's guitar in *Masked & Anonymous*, the name checks in interviews and in *Chronicles*, the attention in *Theme Time Radio Hour*... it's likely that such a verse fragment as *I set my suitcase down* was etched in Dylan's brain by Blind Melon. His poetic brille does the rest; connecting the words to *I been in trouble since* is considerably more powerful (and more poetical) than Blind Lemon's somewhat stiff continuation.

Apparently Boy George, of all people, thinks so too - in the twenty-first century he lovingly steals it for "Wrong" (on *U Can Never B2 Straight*, 2002):

I came to the city with my head so full of dreams
The city was safe alright but not from me
See I've been in trouble since I lay my suitcase down
I love the sound of my own voice, but now I want it drowned

... insinuating that *he* is one of those predators that turn the city into a jungle. Which, given "Boy" George Alan O'Dowd's reputation, indeed does sound a little more convincing from his mouth than from Dylan's.

V Frost in the room, fire in the sky

Got nothin' for you, I had nothin' before
Don't even have anything for myself anymore
Sky full of fire, pain pourin' down
Nothing you can sell me, I'll see you around

In 2007 *DVD Talk* interviews Henry Rollins on the occasion of his forthcoming concert registration *Shock And Awe*. The interview is largely about Rollins' musical heroes, with Rollins acknowledging that he, too, is only a product of his time: *"I'm not saying everything now sucks, but a record that I think is as awesome as Exile On Main Street or Houses Of The Holy? Noooo."*

Recognizable; the impact of music on a receptive individual in his formative years (Rollins is from '61, so about twelve years when those records are released) is never equalled in later years. Yesteryear's music is always better. For, as the German poet Theodor Storm says, *"der Jugend Zauber hängt doch an dir* - the magic of your youth is clung to it".

He actually only knows one exception, Rollins says: the last record by Nick Cave (*Abattoir Blues*, 2004).

> His new collection is extraordinary, it blows the last album away. I wrote him a letter after I played it and said "you and Dylan are like the only guys writing songs right now." I think the last two Dylan records have just been incredible - *Time Out Of Mind* and *Love And Theft*. Those were just amazing.

But a little further on he can explain in a more substantive way what repels him in a lot of recent music, and what he misses:

> But with music, in the 90's something happened to the production where the Pro Tools started coming in, pitch correction started coming in - on rock music. All of a sudden it started to sound contained to me, quantized and contained, and that's just not really what I want from my rock and roll. Where you listen to an older record and you say "yeah those are people in a room, really, really playing". (...) I miss the space, I miss the sound of a guitar in a room where you can hear the air around it. Who makes records like that still? Tom Waits does, Bob Dylan does.

Henry Rollins is an exceptional, tireless multi-talent with an enviable talent for finding the right words, as evidenced by his intelligent, sharp and often witty columns in LA Weekly. And as this interview excerpt shows - a "contained sound" is a clever formulation to express the increasingly sterile sound of rock music. Missing space, "the sound of a guitar in a room where you can hear the air around it" is a perfect, poetic description of the sound Dylan so emphatically seeks when he produces his own records as "Jack Frost".

It's surprisingly close to what Dylan's employees say about the production of *Time Out Of Mind* and *"Love And Theft"*, the sessions that produced "Mississippi". Pianist Jim Dickinson, session musician on *Time Out Of Mind*, remembers:

> One thing that really struck me during those sessions, Dylan, he was standing singing four feet from the microphone, with no earphones on. He was listening to the sound in the room.

And even more right to speak has engineer Chris Shaw, from *"Love And Theft"* to *Trouble No More* Dylan's recording engineer. In the same highly entertaining and informative interview series for *Uncut*, the "Tell Tales Special" on the occasion of the 2008 *Bootleg Series 8* of the same name, Shaw discusses his experiences with Dylan in detail in the studio. "His idea was just, basically", he explains, "get the whole band in the room and get them playing."

Which creates specific problems for a recording engineer, but also explains the "room" sound as Henry Rollins so aptly calls it:

> "And I'd say about 85 per cent of the sound of that record is the band spilling into Bob's microphone, because he'd sing live in the room with the band. Most of the time without headphones. That's why the record has this big, I think, almost kind of swampy sound to it, and he loves it, he really goes for that sound."

But the groundbreaking Dylan researcher Scott Warmuth has an even better explanation for Henry Rollins' outspoken love for particularly those two Dylan records: Rollins hears himself. Or rather: he hears his own words.

Warmuth, who admirably succeeds in tracing sources of Dylan's songs, discovers four fragments in "Mississippi" that Dylan has lifted from Rollins' work. The first one, *your days are numbered*, is arguably somewhat dubious, but the other three are obvious.

In *See A Grown Man Cry*, Warmuth finds:

> *I don't want to know you*
> **I have nothing for you**
> **I don't even have a self for myself anymore**
> *People pick at your body like crows*
> *You want a friend, go hang out with a big rock*
> *It's not me you want*
> *No matter what you think*

See A Grown Man Cry (1992) is an overwhelming work. It consists, like other Rollins works too, of a long series of diary-like notes made by the poet during his many travels, and reveals an extremely sharp observing, eloquent and intelligent mind. Many of the notes express the thoughts of a tormented man who can barely contain his aggression, his frustrations and his senseless hatred, such as:

> *Nijamegan Holland*
> *Forgotten thrown away*
> *Cold raining outside*
> *Hendrix blasting this bar*
> *An asshole in the corner hands pounding the bar off time*
> *I was here five years ago*
> *Watched these guys beat each other up*
> *It was more interesting than the set*
> *Soon the hash bar will open*

...others are philosophical reflections and yet others are actually little more than a situation report, like:

> Germany
> My body is covered with road stench
> Diesel, tobacco, sweat, grease and dirt
> Men's room, rasthaus, no sleep
> I don't want to wash it off
> It's a second skin
> Keeps my back straight
> It insulates me from disease
> Tonight I will sleep with it on

...lyrical in the true sense of the word - expressing feelings - and every note is poetic through and through. The whole (*See A Grown Man Cry* consists of more than a hundred pages filled with this kind of short, pointy notes) is strongly reminiscent of what Dylan reported in the *Fiddler* interview with Martin Bronstein, February 1966, about the creation of his own "Like A Rolling Stone":

> I found myself writing this song, this story, this long piece of vomit about twenty pages long, and out of it I took 'Like a *Rolling* Stone' and made it as a single. And I'd never written anything like that before.

And to Jules Siegel a month later about the same process of creation:

> It was ten pages long," he says. "It wasn't called anything, just a rhythm thing on paper all about my steady hatred directed at some point that was honest. In the end it wasn't hatred, it was telling someone something they didn't know, telling them they were lucky. Revenge, that's a better word.

Vomit, steady hatred, revenge... it sounds like a pointy summary of Rollins' *See A Grown Man Cry*.

The subsequent Old Testament-like verse "Sky full of fire, pain pourin' down" tempts interviewer Gilmore (*Rolling Stone*, 2001) to inquire about Dylan's prophetic qualities. After all, the album *"Love And Theft"* is unfortunately released on 9/11, the day of the attacks on the Twin Towers.

> *Gilmore*: For my part, I've kept circling around a line from *"Mississippi"*: *"Sky full of fire, pain pourin' down."* Is there anything you would like to say about your reaction to the events of that day?
> *Dylan*: One of those Rudyard Kipling poems, "Gentlemen-Rankers," comes to my mind:
>> *We have done with Hope and Honour, we are lost to Love and Truth*
>> *We are dropping down the ladder rung by rung*
>> *And the measure of our torment is the measure of our youth*
>> *God help us, for we knew the worst too young!*

A beautiful, poetic answer, in which Dylan - rightly so - completely fails to address the somewhat embarrassing implication that he would have predictive powers. After all, the choice of words for that ominous verse line is dictated mainly by the sound; two alliterations, inner rhyme and the pleasant rhythm of an anapaest - this truly is a lieder poet's verse line.

VI   Charades

All my powers of expression and thoughts so sublime
Could never do you justice in reason or rhyme
Only one thing I did wrong
Stayed in Mississippi a day too long

Ineradicable, and sometimes tiring, are the many, many Dylan admirers and exegetes who persistently try to interpret Dylan songs biographically. It leads to puzzling with facts and names from the man's life, to often rather embarrassing "analyses" that try to prove that one *you* "actually" is Dylan's wife Sara, another *her* "actually" Joan Baez, and a *baby* in a third song "actually" Edie Sedgwick, or something like that.

In doing so, the puzzlers trivialise - unintentionally, we may assume - Dylan's poetry, downgrading it to petty settlements, childishly encrypted diary entries and small-minded gossip. Inappropriate, and unworthy of a great artist.

Of course; private impressions and personal observations do whirl down into Dylan's work, as with any true artist. You can't describe a train journey poetically if you've never been on a train, you can't describe *jealousy* poetically if you've never experienced this particular emotion, and you must have been confronted at least once with leopard fur and women's hats to be able to use it effectively as an accessory in lyrics. And more than that it is not – "These are images which are just in there and have got to come out," as the writer says in the *SongTalk* interview with Paul Zollo, 1991.

Dylan himself declares since the 60's, following Rimbaud, that *je est un autre*, that the self in his songs is not the same as the writer of the song. As the then only sixteen year old Rimbaud writes in the same *Lettre du Voyant*: "*La chanson est si peu souvent l'oeuvre, c'est-à-dire la pensée chantée et comprise du chanteur* - the song is so rarely the work or the sung thought of the singer himself."

The statement is beautifully illustrated by a witness statement, by Malcom Burn, musician and recording engineer of *Oh Mercy*, in the fascinating *Tell Tale Signs Special* interview series in *Uncut*:

> Nothing on the record took a lot of takes really. The only thing we took a lot of time getting – and this is another interesting thing about is approach – is like, if he was fixing a vocal part. Y'know if he wanted to punch in just a part of a song again. It was never about whether it was in tune or out of tune or anything like that. It would be – let's say he's singing a replacement line – he'd sing it and you'd try to mix it into the original track, he'd listen to it and he'd say, "Ah, nah, nah, nah. That's not the guy." And I'd say, "The guy?" And he'd say, "Yeah. It's not the same guy."

"It's not *the guy*," it's not the person whose character the performer Dylan takes on for this particular song. Burn learns a lot from it, he says. It's not so very important whether a verse sounds a little out of tune, or not quite in time, that doesn't interest Dylan in the least - the personality, "*the guy*" has to be right. It is, in short, acting; *je est un autre*.

So the man who, in these verses of "Mississippi", says that he has such great *powers of expression* and such sublime thoughts, is not Dylan himself. Any doubt about this is definitively dispelled by Elton John, in his disconcerting, very witty and shameless autobiography *Me* (2019):

> Simon and Garfunkel had dinner one night, then played charades. At least, they tried to play charades. They were terrible at it. The best thing I can say about them is that they were better than Bob Dylan. He couldn't get the hang of the 'how many syllables?' thing at all. He couldn't do 'sounds like' either, come to think of it. One of the best lyricists in the world, the greatest man of letters in the history of rock music, and he can't seem to tell you whether a word's got one syllable or two syllables or what it rhymes with! He was so hopeless, I started throwing oranges at him.

Now, Elton's memories aren't necessarily very reliable. This is at a time when Sir Elton Hercules John is a renowned bulk consumer of liquor and drugs, and the orange scene has to be told to him the next morning by others, to his own horror, but the core of the story, Dylan's clumsiness at a game of Charades, must be true.

Still, Elton acknowledges the greatness of Dylan's lyrics. He surely recognizes the tenor of these verses, of

All my powers of expression and thoughts so sublime
Could never do you justice in reason or rhyme.

After all, the Rocketman himself has had a Dylan song on the shelf for years, for which he just can't find the right *je-ne-sais-quoi*:

> There are words that Bernie's written that I've never managed to come up with music for. He wrote a great lyric called "The Day That Bobby Went Electric", about hearing Dylan sing "Subterranean Homesick Blues" for the first time, and I just couldn't get a tune I thought was right; I tried four or five times.

Probably early 1980, for the *21 At 33* album. The leaked demo is actually quite nice, but is not about "Subterranean Homesick Blues". Elton's regular lyricist Bernie Taupin closes in the last verse:

> *The day that Bobby went electric*
> *I was struggling through my teens*
> *And when he plugged in up at Newport*
> *I was caught up in a dream*

... so that must have been "Maggie's Farm".

As far as the content of these "Mississippi" lines is concerned, the message is not too earth-shattering, obviously. "There are no words to describe your beauty" is actually a rather corny compliment. And the easy way out for the failing poet, who, after all, is paid to find the words to describe beauty, feelings, emotion at all. Still: Sarah Vaughan's "Words Can't Describe"; "I Don't Know How To Say I Love You" by The Superlatives; Sinatra's "How Deep Is The Ocean?"... it is of all times and apparently even the biggest guns do have the odd off-day – and then turn need into a virtue, creating from the search for the right words a masterpiece that thematises exactly that very speechlessness. Shakespeare, of course ("Shall I compare thee to a summer's day?"), Goethe's *Werther*, Rimbaud (*"ne sachant m'expliquer sans paroles païennes, je voudrais me taire - unaware how to express myself without pagan words, I'd rather be mute"*)... and Dylan, of course.

In an uninspired past, the bard has sought refuge in that same escape route. In "Never Say Goodbye" for example:

You're beautiful beyond words
You're beautiful to me

As well, in a sad variant, in the mean "Ballad In Plain D" ("The words to say I'm sorry, I haven't found yet") - but there it is still more beautifully, poetically phrased than in "Never Say Goodbye". And again, in the twenty-first century, Dylan does find another poetically successful way of saying that he doesn't know what to say: *I'm searching for phrases to sing your praises* ("Soon After Midnight", 2012).

And the same paradoxical achievement comes from *the guy* from "Mississippi", thanks to screenwriter Dylan: he finds great words to say he can't find words.

VII Dorsey Dixon

Well, the devil's in the alley, mule's in the stall
Say anything you wanna, I have heard it all
I was thinkin' 'bout the things that Rosie said
I was dreaming I was sleepin' in Rosie's bed

Rowland Sherman is the photographer who will later take the famous picture of Dylan used for *Greatest Hits*. "With that blue light, with the white halo," as Sherman says, adding:

> And it won a Grammy Award! I didn't think much of it, but now it turns out that that shot is one of the icons of the '60s. Quite proud of it, but at the time I didn't think it was that big of a deal.

 That picture was taken in Washington in 1965, but Sherman already knew Dylan for a long time. He's there, 28 July 1963 at the Newport Folk Festival, when the scruffy vagabond is catapulted by Joan Baez and becomes the new king of folk music. That's how the photographer sees it, anyway:

There was a crowd of maybe 60 or 100 people. And then Joan Baez sat in with him, and all of a sudden the crowd was two or three hundred people. It was all his stuff, and she was singing the harmonies to them. Fabulous stuff. The crowd got bigger and bigger, and everyone was enthralled. It was because if Baez is singing with this guy, he must have something.

And at the end of the weekend, when Pete Seeger, Peter, Paul & Mary, The Freedom Singers and Joan Baez form his background choir on "Blowin' In The Wind", it is evident: Dylan is the star, "he was untouchable".

Dylan's presence is also fairly prominent in the 32-page program booklet. One and a half pages with an ode-like contribution he wrote about folk artist, harmonica player and music critic Tony "Little Sun" Glover ("- for Dave Glover"), the lyrics of "Blowin' In The Wind", and so on. Yet Dylan is not on the record that will be released six months later, *Old Time Music At Newport (Recorded Live At The Newport Folk Festival 1963)* - a strange blunder from record label Vanguard, which still does have complete, officially unreleased, recordings of every Dylan appearance that weekend.

An interesting record it is nevertheless - if only because it reveals a few sources of Dylan's later repertoire. The young Dylan (he's 22 by then) kept his ears and eyes open for three days, visited the workshops and attended the performances, and that record was probably on his turntable too.

The LP opens with four songs by Doc Watson, the man from whom Dylan learned "Naomi Wise", and "Lonesome Road Blues", "Freight Train Blues" and "Lone Pilgrim", "Handsome

Molly" and "Little Maggie", the songs, in short, which lay the foundation of his oeuvre and which he still has on a pedestal today.

The same goes for the artist and the repertoire of the next artist on that Newport record: Clarence Ashley. Another admired musician who Dylan meets and hears playing in the Village, and here Ashley performs his version of "Little Sadie", the version that a few years later, on *Self Portrait* (1970), seems to be the template for Dylan's recording.

Similar aha-moments delivers Side 2, with the legend Dock Boggs. Boggs, whose "Danville Girl" in the 80s via the detour "New Danville Girl" will lead to "Brownsville Girl", here plays his classic "Sugar Baby", the namesake of the brilliant finale of *"Love And Theft"* (2001).

And in between, between Dock Boggs and Clarence 'Tom' Ashley, opening Side 2, the under-appreciated Dorsey Dixon shines.

The invitation to perform at Newport is a late, meagre recognition of Dorsey Dixon's forgotten music historical importance. Born in 1897 in Darlington, South Carolina, Dorsey has worked in the local textile factory since he was twelve, as do his father and his six siblings. Sister Nancy has been a spinster since she was eight, and brother Howard has been on the loom since his tenth birthday.

Dorsey and Howard are musical, they perform and make their own songs about their lives in the factory, the miserable living conditions and the exploitation by the manufacturers. Locally known, popular at demonstrations and trade union activities, but they don't make money with it. At the age of forty, Dorsey still works in a textile factory, now fifty miles away, in East Rockingham.

In 1936 a gruesome car accident happens near the factory, in which two fellow locals are killed. Dorsey sees the car wreck, the blood and the shrapnel. He writes a song about it, "Wreck On The Highway" (though he originally calls the song "I Didn't Hear Nobody Pray"). The song penetrates the canon quite smoothly:

> *Who did you say it was brother?*
> *Who was it fell by the way?*
> *When whiskey and blood run together*
> *Did you hear anyone pray?*
>
> *I didn't hear nobody pray, dear brother*
> *I didn't hear nobody pray*
> *I heard the crash on the highway*
> *But, I didn't hear nobody pray*

But it won't make the Dixons rich either. Howard and Dorsey are allowed to record sixty songs for record company Victor, but business-wise they don't have a clue, of course. A&R guy Eli Oberstein sells the copyrights of all of them. Roy Acuff hits the jackpot with "Wreck On The Highway" and scores a big hit (the ungrammatical double denial in the original title is considered too rustic). Unscrupulously and speciously, Acuff puts his name under the song, and only years later, when Dixon finds out he did miss out on quite a lot of money, he sends in a lawyer. In 1946 he gets the copyrights back, an unknown percentage of "future royalties" plus $1,700 - a pittance.

It takes until the end of the 50s - Dorsey is already in his sixties - when some recognition comes up. His songs are discovered by folkies, in 1961 he is given the opportunity to record an album (*Babies In The Mill* - the title song is, obviously, about the disgraceful practices of child labour in American textile factories, in the first half of the twentieth century) and Pete Seeger introduces him at his first major performance, at the Newport Folk Festival in 1963.

Dylan's in the audience and pays close attention. Dorsey (brother Howard died in 1961) opens with his bitterly comical "Intoxicated Rat", which is on the repertoire of Doc Watson, Cisco Houston and The New Lost City Ramblers, and - sure enough - even on Brook Benton's.

Then Dixon plays his big hit, which he now calls "Wreck On The Highway" too, and finally he performs his "first blues" (as he says himself), "Weave Room Blues" which he wrote more than thirty years ago, in 1931. In the 30s that song is on the repertoire of every trade union activity around the textile factories, sometimes in the variant "Cotton Mill Blues", but no one knows it was written by Dorsey Dixon. Pete Seeger sings it, The New Lost City Ramblers record it in 1961 for their hit album *Vol. 3*, but even in the standard work *American Folk Songs Of Protest* by the highly educated John Greenway (1953), in which the song is extensively discussed, Dorsey's name is not mentioned.

His work will stand the test of time, though. Dylan does his bit and takes that beautiful image *devil's in your alley* to the twenty-first century, to "Mississippi":

I've got the blues, I've got the blues,
I've got them awful weave-room blues;
I got the blues, the weave-room blues.

Harness eyes are breaking with the doubles coming through,
Devil's in your alley and he's coming after you,
Our hearts are aching, well, let's take a little booze;
For we're simply dying with them weave-room blues.

Newport, and the recognition by greats like Seeger, Cisco Houston and The New Lost City Ramblers, comes too late for Dixon. He's half-blind, old, has a few heart attacks in '64, has to move in with his son in Florida and dies in 1968.

Thus, he again misses out on a shipload of money four years later, when Roy Acuff's version of "Wreck On The Highway" is released on The Nitty Gritty Dirt Band's platinum hit record *Will The Circle Be Unbroken*. On which - finally - the song is not attributed to Roy Acuff anymore. But erroneously, to add insult to injury, to a "Dorothy" Dixon.

The devil was in the alley again, probably.

VIII Pretty Maids All In A Row

Well, the devil's in the alley, mule's in the stall
Say anything you wanna, I have heard it all
I was thinkin' 'bout the things that Rosie said
I was dreaming I was sleepin' in Rosie's bed

 "I didn't really have to grapple much. It's the kind of thing where you pile up stream-of-consciousness verses and then leave it alone and come pull things out." That's what Dylan says in response to "I Contain Multitudes" in the 12 June 2020 *New York Times* interview.

It is a pleasant, worth reading interview with a grand old man reflecting on his own work with attractive modesty and a strange mix of wonder plus resignation. We were already familiar with the tenor of his self-analysis; in earlier interviews Dylan often tells us that he has no idea where those songs come from. But by now he is almost eighty and chooses his words more soberly than ever - and at the same time with a kind of self-evident acceptance of the magic behind them. He calls his creative phase "trance writing", he doesn't plan his songs, songs come "out of the blue, out of thin air", and:

The songs seem to know themselves and they know that I can sing them, vocally and rhythmically. They kind of write themselves and count on me to sing them.

Beautifully phrased, with a charming touch of mysticism - but meanwhile the old bard really could add the proviso that the songs do not come *entirely* "out of the blue" or "out of thin air". That the "songs seem to know themselves" has a rather earthy explanation: large parts of his songs already exist. For decades, usually.

So, in this verse "devil in the alley" comes from Dorsey Dixon, and most other words don't come falling from the sky either, but from other people's songs.

"Mule's in the stall" Dylan borrows - consciously or unconsciously - from an old acquaintance, from Howlin' Wolf, from "Evil (Is Goin' On)":

> *Well, long way from home and*
> *Can't sleep at all*
> *You know another mule*
> *Is kickin' in your stall*

Written by Willie Dixon and recorded by Howlin' Wolf as early as 1954, but in '69 he scored his last hit with a re-recording of the song. It's a cool swinging Chicago blues from which Dylan will also lend the sound and stomp, for songs like "Lonesome Day Blues" and "Cry A While", for example.

The "blue" out of which *I was thinkin' 'bout the things that Rosie said* seems to fall is somewhat more unlikely, at least until 2020, when Dylan lists his long list of request numbers in part 4 of "Murder Most Foul". Apart from usual suspects like

"The Long, Lonesome Road", John Lee Hooker, "Mystery Train" and "I'd Rather Go Blind", the narrator requests DJ Wolfman Jack to play surprising, undylanesque songs like Queen's "Another One Bites The Dust" and Beethoven, and in between, among those surprising requests is equally striking: "Play Don Henley - play Glen Frey".

Interviewer Douglas Brinkley did notice it too, and in that *New York Times* article he enquires:

> DB: *Your mention of Don Henley and Glenn Frey on "Murder Most Foul" came off as a bit of a surprise to me. What Eagles songs do you enjoy the most?*
> BD: "New Kid in Town," "Life in the Fast Lane," "Pretty Maids All in a Row." That could be one of the best songs ever.

Every artist in the world will be particularly flattered when one of his songs is awarded by Bob Dylan as "one of the best songs ever", but it's a bit sad for Joe Walsh that Dylan seems to think it's a Henley and Frey song - this is the only song from *Hotel California* that was written by Walsh (although he also gets a co-credit for the guitar lick of "Life In The Fast Lane"). As a consolation: the list of songs that the Nobel Prize winner calls "one of the best songs ever" is already a few pages long.

Still, a bit mysterious Dylan's praise is; the bard undoubtedly belongs to a very small minority of music lovers who will regard "Pretty Maids All In A Row" so highly - indeed, few people will find it even the *album's* best song. Objectively, if that is possible at all, songs like "Hotel California" or, say, "The Last Resort" are just better songs.

Anyway, it seems to have animated Dylan to follow the men's solo careers as well, and the otherwise rather insignificant "I Got Love" of Glen Frey's solo album *The Allnighter* (1984) apparently kept wavering in the thin air:

Jumped on the freeway with this song in my head
I started thinkin' 'bout the things we said
I said I'm sorry; She said I'm sorry too;
You know I can't be happy 'less I'm happy with you.

...from which both that *thinkin' about the things we said* and *I said I'm sorry; she said I'm sorry too* seem to descend into "Mississippi". Surprising, yet in line with other unlikely sources for Dylan's production - such as a Japanese gangster epic, obscure nineteenth-century poets and a 1961 *Time* magazine.

The closing lines of this quatrain, in which a certain "Rosie" is sung, more or less bring the song "home"- after all, the refrain line of the poem originates from the song recorded by Lomax, from "Rosie".

In the same 2020 New York Times interview, Dylan reveals how he writes "most of my recent songs", yet again in response to "I Contain Multitudes". Not only the qualification *trance writing* stands out, but also Dylan's own analysis of the trigger for those stream-of-consciousness verses:

"In that particular song, the last few verses came first. So that's where the song was going all along. Obviously, the catalyst for the song is the title line. It's one of those where you write it on instinct. Kind of in a trance state."

This is about a song he (presumably) writes in 2020. But it seems to apply one-on-one to a song he wrote a quarter of a century earlier, to "Mississippi". Just like Dylan uses the lines with the Walt Whitman quote as a starting point for "I Contain Multitudes", the obvious starting point here is Lomax' *Only one thing I did wrong / Stayed in Mississippi a day too long* - and then the stream-of-consciousness starts to flow.

"Rosie" bubbling up halfway is, all in all, not that surprising anymore.

IX   Abandon all hope

Walkin' through the leaves, falling from the trees
Feelin' like a stranger nobody sees
So many things that we never will undo
I know you're sorry, I'm sorry too

 The opening line of this quatrain is deceptive. At first sight, the setting looks like a clichéd film scene. A melancholy protagonist, strolling in an autumnal forest over the rustling leaf. It is only at second glance one is struck by this atypical *falling*.

The narrator does not walk through *fallen* leaves, fallen from the trees, but through leaves, *falling* from the trees. *Participium praesens*, a present participle: the leaves are falling, while the protagonist walks through them - the protagonist who does feel like an invisible stranger here... suddenly this is very reminiscent of Dante.

"Canto III" from Dante's *Inferno* is probably the best known. It is the song that tells how Dante and Virgil arrive at the Gates of Hell, at the cheerful welcome sign *Lasciate ogni speranza, voi ch'intrate* – "Abandon all hope, ye who enter here" - the closing words Dylan re-uses in 2020 for "Crossing The Rubicon" (*I painted my wagon, abandoned all hope and I crossed the Rubicon*), just as further verses seem inspired by that same excerpt from the *Divina Commedia*:

> You won't find any happiness here
> No happiness or joy

Hell's vestibule already is an ordeal to Dante. And here are still only the souls of those who have been neither good nor bad - but their screams, the "languages divers, *orribili favelle,* horrible words" and the "words of agony" frighten Dante. They have to make their way through though, to the "the dismal shore of the Acheron", the muddy, black, bitter River of Suffering, where ferryman Charon will sail them to the other side, to the underworld.

Dante's description of Charon, especially Charon's eyes, suggests that Dylan has browsed the *Inferno* more than once and more than fleetingly. The first time the ferryman is described is in this song, in verse 82-99. The introduction ends remarking that the skipper has *"wheels of fire around the eyes"*, the title of one of Dylan's Basement songs from 1967.

The second time is ten lines down:

> The dæmon, with eyes like burning coal,
> - Charon – enrols them, for the passage bound
> And with his oar goads on each lingering soul

"Eyes like burning coal", as Wordsworth translates *con occhi di bragia* seems to echo in "Tangled Up In Blue":

> *Then she opened up a book of poems*
> *And handed it to me*
> *Written by an Italian poet*
> *From the thirteenth century*
> *And every one of them words rang true*
> *And glowed like burnin' coal*

Probably one of the most discussed verses in Dylan's oeuvre, but on which a kind of consensus has gradually emerged. The obvious candidates for this "Italian poet from the thirteenth century" are the fourteenth-century poets Petrarch, Boccaccio and Dante, and the scales tip towards to Dante (although in '78 Dylan clouded the waters by answering when asked: "Plutarch. Was that his name?"). However, the ease with which Dylan, in live performances, changes the reference in question to *Baudelaire* or to *Jeremiah* does give ground to the theory that the bard has no particular poet in mind at all, but in this verse line, as is often the case, chooses the *sound*.

Inferno, the first part of the *Divine Comedy*, then seems to provide decor, imagery and colour for this quatrain in "Mississippi". In *Chronicles*, Dylan in any case parades his memory that he had the book in his hands:

> Sometimes I'd open up a book and see a handwritten note scribbled in the front, like in Machiavelli's *The Prince,* there was written, "The spirit of the hustler." "The cosmopolitan man" was written on the title page in Dante's *Inferno*.

This plays in one of his lodgings, with "Ray and Chloe", in the time before Dylan recorded his first LP, so around 1960. It seems rather unlikely that the autobiographer Dylan remembers handwritten scribbles in other people's books more than forty years later, but well alright. In this passage Dylan sums up a whole zip of antique and less antique writers, refers to works that do not exist and remembers fantasised titles - apparently Dylan is not so much striving for academic correctness, but still does feel a need to demonstrate that he is not entirely uneducated.

Anyway - *Inferno*. After that depressing vestibule Dante and Virgil approach the bank of the Acheron. Charon sees that Dante is still alive and therefore doesn't want to take him with him, but is overruled by Virgil, who seems to have some authority, down here. Meanwhile, it gets busier and busier on the bank: the souls of the damned, who have to be taken to the other side.

> *As in the autumn-time the leaves fall off,*
> *First one and then another, till the branch*
> *Unto the earth surrenders all its spoils;*
> *In similar wise the evil seed of Adam*
> *Throw themselves from that margin one by one,*
> *At signals, as a bird unto its lure.*

And thus, Dante is walking *through the leaves, falling from the trees*, through the wandering souls who can't see him, to Charon's ferry. He's a stranger here, being the only one with a *good soul*, according to Virgil, among all those souls who *never will undo* their failed lives. Dante's sorry. And they are sorry too.

X   Eyesight To The Blind

Some people will offer you their hand and some won't
Last night I knew you, tonight I don't
I need somethin' strong to distract my mind
I'm gonna look at you 'til my eyes go blind

 More than halfway the song and it gets harder and harder to follow Dylan's claim from that Rolling Stone interview, about the song touching on the Declaration of Independence, the Constitution and the Bill of Rights. And it's increasingly understandable that producer Lanois argues for "sexy and more sexy".

The narrator is emotional and at the very least suggests that his current feelings of regret and loss are due to a recent break-up. In the blues jargon of Howlin' Wolf and Willie Dixon, *the mule in the stall* is a love rival, the man with whom your wife has just deceived you. The narrator worries about the things "Rosie" said and dreams of lying in "Rosie's" bed again. And now he's wandering around like a stranger, dazed and confused, regretting the things that can't be undone, and presuming that "you" has regrets too... no, it's quite easy to follow how Lanois hears a sultry love drama between the lines.

That doesn't get any less in this verse.

Genesis 38 is a somewhat lust-filled, ruthless, and farcical intermezzo in the Bible's first book. The chapter tries to bring some order to the chaotic family history of Judah, the fourth Founding Father of the Tribes. Judah's first son Er is "wicked", so God has to kill him, unfortunately. Brother Onan then has to fulfill his obligations and impregnate Er's widow, but he prefers to spill his seed on the rocks. Beep beep, Jack, you're dead (*"And the thing which he did displeased the Lord: wherefore he slew him also"*). Which means, subsequently: another widow to take care of. All right, says Judah to this fresh widow, his daughter-in-law Tamar, when my third son will be old enough, you shall be his wife.

But Judah forgets, or changes his mind. Tamar works all these years in his household but does not get a husband - not even that third son, who is old enough by now. Then comes the farcical element: Tamar "covered her with a vail" and, masked and anonymous, stands whorishly "by the way to Timnath", where her father-in-law passes by a little later. He thinks he sees an attractive harlot and wants to "come in unto her". He can't pay now, but gives his signet ring, cord and staff as pledge. When Judah returns to pay, Tamar and his pledge are gone.

A few months later his daughter-in-law Tamar turns out to be pregnant. So obviously, she has to die, because that's how it's supposed to be. But then Tamar shows the things of the man who has impregnated her: signet ring, cord and staff. This puts Judah in his place. "She hath been more righteous than I." *And he knew her again no more.*

It is the fourth time in Genesis that *knew* is used in the sense of having intercourse. That's how Daniel Lanois hears Dylan using it in "Mississippi": "Last night I knew you, tonight I don't" - and in that case it may indeed sound *sexy and more sexy.*

Hardly "constitutional" or "Bill Of Rights", but equally erotic, or at least amorous, is the desperate follow-up. Word choice now seems to be inspired by the blues canon again, although the well-versed may also think of Samson - who remained in love with Delilah, after all, until his eyes were gouged out. More obvious, however, is Aleck "Rice" Miller, better known as Sonny Boy Williamson II.

Sonny Boy Williamson comes from Mississippi, which may be a trigger, but the harmonica virtuoso is a constant in Dylan's oeuvre anyway. The bard quotes Williamson in songs like "Outlaw Blues", copies "Don't Start Me Talkin" for the throwaway "Stop Now" (of which he then literally takes the chorus from Williamson's "Stop Now Baby"), and Dylan plays the same "Don't Start Me Talkin'" with The Plugz in the David Letterman Show, 1984.

In *Chronicles*, the autobiographer dreams up the story how Sonny Boy gave him a harmonica lesson once ("Boy, you play too fast"); in *Theme Time Radio Hour*, radio maker Dylan plays no less than eight of his songs and his later songs are stuffed with references too; "Your Funeral And My Trial" in "Cry A While", for example, and in "Spirit On The Water" the Nobel Prize winner quotes both from "Black Gal Blues" and "Sugar Mama Blues".

Here, in "Mississippi", Dylan chooses a reversal of Sonny Boy's immortal classic "Eyesight To The Blind":

You're talking about your woman,
I wish to God, man, that you could see mine
You're talking about your woman,
I wish to God that you could see mine
Every time the little girl start to loving,
She bring eyesight to the blind

It seems to be some sort of a personal matter for Williamson, by the way. "Born Blind", "Don't Lose Your Eye", "Unseeing Eye"... quite a few songs from his catalogue lack the light in the eyes.

His most famous in that category, "Eyesight To The Blind", he does record a few times himself (among others, with Willie Dixon and with Elmore James), and appears on the records and setlists of big guns like B.B. King, Eric Clapton, Mose Allison, Gary Moore and Aerosmith. Officially promoted to rock history, the song is in 1969, by Pete Townshend for *Tommy*, of course. Though the biggest hit with it was scored by The Larks in 1951 (Top 10 in the R&B charts), which is perhaps one of the best arrangements indeed.

But Dylan's reversal is the cleverest variant; Sonny Boy's blind can see again when she "starts to loving", with Dylan the seeing "therefore" become blind when she stops loving again, when the love is over.

XI   Bonnie Blue

Well I got here followin' the southern star
I crossed that river just to be where you are
Only one thing I did wrong
Stayed in Mississippi a day too long

 One of the few successful songs on one of Dylan's weakest albums, *Down In The Groove* (1988) is his version of the old folk song "Shenandoah". It *is*, of course, a beautiful nineteenth century song by itself - almost impossible to ruin.

The origin of "Shenandoah" is unclear. Alan Lomax guesses it's a sea-shanty, an old sailor's song of French-Canadian origin, probably originated around 1810. Given the lyrics, other musicologists conclude, it might be a "river-shanty", deriving its name from the Shenandoah River in Virginia. Why then the protagonist repeatedly sings he has to cross the *Missouri* River is unexplained, though — that particular river is almost a thousand miles away. "Shenandoah" is a singing, melodious name, that's probably the best explanation.

Oh Shenandoah, I love your daughter
Look away, you rollin' river
It was for her I'd cross the water.
Look away, we're bound away
Across the wide Missouri

Dylan sings the version in which the narrator so desperately seeks to reach "Sally", across the wide Missouri, and she is the "daughter of Shenandoah". Which could indicate an Indian tribe, or the name of the river where she lives, or, in the literal interpretation, the name of his future father-in-law. "Oh Shenandoah, I love your daughter," after all.

The Indian tribe-option is by far the most attractive to lay a line to "Mississippi". The Senedos, a tribe along the Shenandoah River, are the obvious candidates - all the more so since *Shenandoah* in their language means "daughter of the stars". *Following the star, I crossed the river.* Coincidence, of course, but certainly a nice coincidence.

The real link, however, is that ancient image of "crossing a river", the metaphor to represent the effort the man makes to reach the woman of his dreams. We sang that already in the Middle Ages:

There were two royal children,
Their love was turned to grief.
They could not come together
The water was too deep.

The "Song of the Two Royal Children", about the regal kids who are not allowed to see each other. One king puts his daughter in the monastery, on the banks of the wide river. She puts a candle on the balustrade at night so that the king's son on the other bank can orient himself as he swims towards her, in pitch darkness. An "evil nun" blows out the candle when he is halfway, the king's son drowns, and when his beloved finds the body the next morning, she commits suicide out of desperation.

A familiar story which, of course, goes back to the age-old Greek myth *Hero and Leander*, the story that inspired hundreds of artists from Antiquity to the twenty-first century - it's an ancient, popular and ineradicable image, the river separating lovers. Or as a metaphor for every figurative meaning of "border" at all; it is no coincidence that *watershed* is synonymous with *milestone, radical event, turning point*. Which is how the poet Dylan uses *river* throughout his entire oeuvre. From "Watching The River Flow" to "Baby, Stop Crying" and from "Man In The Long Black Coat" to "Moonlight" and "Crossing The Rubicon"; the rivers symbolize turning points.

In "Mississippi" Dylan gives it an extra, mythical touch; the narrator follows the *southern star* that leads him to that turning point. Mythical, as a Southern star does not exist - unlike a North Star, Polaris, there is no fixed star in the southern sky. A less romantically inclined astronomer might argue that the Sun is "the star in the south", but in the arts it's usually a nickname (for a special diamond, for example, as in the film *The Southern Star* with Orson Welles and an Ursula Andress at her most beautiful, 1969).

It's not really a household name, though.

Presumably the poet wants to avoid digressing - after all, the *star* in any other wind direction has additional meanings or associations. The Star in the East leads to the Child Jesus, the North Star, which is shining too in one of Joni Mitchell's breath-taking songs, "This Flight Tonight",

> *"Look out the left," the captain said*
> *"The lights down there, that's where we'll land"*
> *Saw a falling star burning*
> *High above the Las Vegas sand*
>
> *It wasn't the one that you gave to me*
> *That night down south between the trailers*
> *Not the early one that you wish upon*
> *Not the northern one that guides in the sailors*

...is an age-old orientation point. And a *Western Star* conjures up completely different images, obviously. So, all that's left is a "safe", a neutral *southern* star. At most it pushes the associations, especially in the light of Dylan's enigmatic statement that the song is about "the Declaration of Independence, the Constitution and the Bill of Rights", towards the Civil War, to the *Bonnie Blue Flag* hoisted on the Capitol Dome of Mississippi in 1861.

That flag consists of a single, large, "Southern" star on a blue field. In the South it is popular, a hastily written song perpetuates its popularity and promotes the flag to become the first unofficial flag of the Confederate States of America:

> *We are a band of brothers, and native to the soil,*
> *Fighting for our liberty with treasure, blood, and toil;*
> *And when our rights were threatened, the cry rose near and far,*
> *Hurrah! for the Bonnie Blue Flag, that bears a single star.*

The song is sung in *Gods And Generals* (2003), the film for which Dylan writes the brilliant "Cross The Green Mountain" (well after "Mississippi") and the cinephile Dylan will have noticed the song earlier in *Gone With The Wind* - Rhett Butler lovingly calls his daughter Bonnie "Bonnie Blue", Melanie (Olivia de Havilland) says her eyes are "blue as the Bonnie Blue Flag".

Too bad the movie's in Georgia. And not in Mississippi.

XII   Roses Of Yesterday

Well my ship's been split to splinters and it's sinkin' fast
I'm drownin' in the poison, got no future, got no past
But my heart is not weary, it's light and it's free
I've got nothin' but affection for all those who've sailed with me

For many fans of the song the favourite quatrain. The opening *accumulatio* indeed has a crushing, pleasantly archaic and terrifying visual power (plus a cheap, yet irresistible alliteration in *split to splinters*) - but the exceptional beauty of these four lines is due to the contrast, to the completely unexpected and beautifully poetic change to gentleness and bonhomie in the third line.

"Willkommen und Abschied" (*Welcome and Farewell*) is the best known of Goethe's so-called *Sesenheimer Lieder*, a collection of poems to which Goethe contributes around the age of twenty-one. The young law student then lives in Strasbourg and befriends the theologian and art theorist Herder. Johann Gottfried Herder is only five years older, but he becomes Goethe's literary mentor, teaches him Rousseau, Shakespeare and Homer and opens his eyes to the beauty of *Volkslieder*, of folk songs. Goethe already had some literary ambition - and now it's taking shape. The inspiration, lastly, lives forty kilometres away, in the Alsace village of Sessenheim: the eighteen-year-old minister's daughter Friederike Brion.

 The two remaining Friederike portraits do not really reveal her attraction, but apparently there is something about her - after Goethe has left Friederike, the young poet Jakob Lenz, who is just as madly in love, reports for duty. Lenz will write the remaining *Sesenheimer Lieder*.

Goethe's genius awakes here and now, in the poems he writes being in love with Friederike. In "*Willkommen und Abschied*", the young *Sturm & Drang* poet lyrically recounts how he does not think, but rather acts, on a whim, jumping on his horse late at night and galloping out of town, through the dark forest, the forty kilometres to Friederike. The second verse reveals his affinity with the narrator of "Mississippi":

> From out a hill of clouds the moon
> Mournful gaze through the mist:
> The winds their soft wings flutter'd soon,
> And in my ear horribly hissed;
> The night a thousand ghouls had made,
> Yet fresh and joyous was my mind;
> What fire within my veins then play'd!
> What glow was in my heart shrin'd!

Darkness and horror, *yet fresh and joyous was my mind*. The secret of this untouched, uncluttered mind is clear: the narrator is in love, is wearing his rose-coloured glasses, is on his way to his lover - by whom he is indeed welcomed "with tenderness" in the next verse.

At Dylan's protagonist, the source of his "light and free heart" is less unambiguous. If this verse had stood alone, it would unmistakably be a death scene. "*My ship's been split to splinters and it's sinkin' fast*" would then be something like "my life is done" or "my soul is leaving me", just as the Dantesque "*drowning in the poison*" evokes a life farewell rather than an "ordinary" gloomy, pessimistic state of mind.

Appropriate then is the closing line, in which the narrator speaks mild, resigned and summarizing deathbed words: "*I've got nothin' but affection for all those who've sailed with me*".

Only the beautiful, aphoristic *got no future, got no past* fits less supple in such an interpretation. It seems to derive from that corny inspirational quote, which gets new life thanks to *Kung Fu Panda* (2008). It is the aphorism the old Master Oogway, the guru-like turtle, shares with Panda Po in the face of his approaching death:

> *Yesterday is history,*
> *Tomorrow is a mystery,*
> *Today is a gift -*
> *That's why we call it the present*

Corny enough to brighten up kitchen tiles, calligraphed wall posters and Facebook statuses of unimaginative house mothers, and does indeed approximate something like *no future, no past*. By the way, it is attributed rather stubbornly to Alice Morse Earle, the American historian and writer, and would then have come from her fascinating study *Sun-Dials and Roses of Yesterday* (1902), but really cannot be found therein.

More obvious is that the poet Dylan incorporates an echo of his Bible studies, the same notion he already incorporated in "Born In Time": that God and Jesus were always there, "outside of time", and Jesus is born *in time* only for those few earthly years. God, as Dylan learned at the Bible study, is an Eternal Being – He has no past and no future, being "outside of time".

However, to extend the impact of these words to "Mississippi" goes far too far; it would imply that the I-person, who with these words places himself outside of Time, imagines himself divine. No, this verse fragment is probably another example of "words that just come up", as Dylan often says about his own song writing. Like in the conversation with Happy Traum:

> "There are times you just pick up an instrument – something will come, like a tune or some kind of wild line will come into your head and you'll develop that. If it's a tune on a piano or guitar - you'll just *uuuuuuhhhh* [humming] whatever it brings out in the voice, you'll write those words down. And they might not mean anything to you at all, and you just go on, and that will be what happens."

That's what Dylan says in 1968, and almost half a century later he repeats it in slightly different words in his Nobel Prize acceptance speech:

> I don't have to know what a song means. I've written all kinds of things into my songs. And I'm not going to worry about it – what it all means.

And somewhere in between, between 1968 and 2016, he records "Mississippi", in which he also writes *all kinds of things*. Like *got no future, got no past*.

I don't know what it means, either. But it sounds good. And you want your songs to sound good.

XIII Down In The Groove

Everybody movin' if they ain't already there
Everybody got to move somewhere
Stick with me baby, stick with me anyhow
Things should start to get interestin' right about now

"What would I say if I met Dylan?" His answer, in keeping with his stylish image, is elegant: "I hope you don't mind."

 Bryan Ferry is being interviewed for his Dylan album *Dylanesque* (2007), a tribute project arousing rather diverging opinions. The title is a red rag: the Dylan covers by Ferry, the grand master of irony, are anything but Dylanesque - smooth polished, tastefully arranged, wrinkle-free produced... in short, Ferry-esque. Hardcore Dylan fans are rarely tolerant of covers anyway, but the less rabid fans also miss the rough and rowdy, the jagged edges and the raw emotion.

However, the more neutral listeners are generally positive. Also because songs like "Simple Twist Of Fate" and "Just Like Tom Thumb's Blues" have a magical, sheer indestructible power - they are almost impossible to mess up. And Ferry's adaptation of "Positively Fourth Street" actually has an enriching quality. The acoustic package (piano and Spanish guitar, mainly) plus Ferry's somewhat plaintive, high pitched vocals do have an unreal, alienating effect; the contrast of the graceful recitation with the mean, snarling lyrics is fascinating.

Anyhow, it's quite likely that the bard at that fictional meeting with Roxy Music's old foreman would say: "I most certainly don't mind. On the contrary."

Ferry has been lining Dylan's pockets since 1973, when the single from his first solo album *These Foolish Things*, an equally alienating version of "A Hard Rain's A-Gonna Fall", became a big hit. The royalties for "It Ain't Me, Babe" from the successor *Another Time, Another Place* - again gold - and "It's All Over Now, Baby Blue" and "Don't Think Twice" from the well-selling album *Frantic* (2002) are not bad either and are increased fivefold by the equally well-selling *Dylanesque*.

Apart from that financially motivated, obvious approval from the master, Dylan might also have artistic appreciation. Dylan repeatedly confesses, both in *Chronicles* and in interviews as well as in his *MusiCares* speech, his gratitude and sympathy for all his colleagues who cover his songs. Bryan Ferry probably even has an edge.

The contemporaries (Dylan is four years older) largely share a same musical taste, the same missionary drive and even an overlapping choice of repertoire. Years before Dylan's "Sinatra albums" Ferry already has success with his declaration of love to the same American Songbook, the gold-scoring *As Time Goes By* (1999).

This shared, wide-ranging taste is perhaps best noticeable on Ferry's third solo album, *Let's Stick Together* (1976). A tasteful adaptation of the long-standing "You Go To My Head", which Dylan will record for *Triplicate* forty years later, "Shame, Shame, Shame" from Jimmy Reed, sung on *Rough And Rowdy Ways*, Ferry's own ode to Dylan's cast-iron art motto "Re-make/Re-model" (*"next time is the best time, we all know"*), his ode to Humphrey Bogart ("2HB") and the opening song, the song with which Ferry scores his biggest solo hit: "Let's Stick Together".

Dylan chooses "Let's Stick Together" as the opening track for his maligned album *Down In The Groove* (1988) and most music lovers will agree that Dylan does not match the excitement, drive and pure musical pleasure that bursts from Ferry's arrangement. Or from the original, by Wilbert Harrison, 1962.

Wilbert Harrison has earned his ticket to the rock 'n' roll Olympus three years earlier, with "Kansas City" - the song from which Dylan lovingly steals for "Just Like Tom Thumb's Blues" (*they got some hungry women there* is a hardly disguised derivative from Wilbert's *they got some crazy women there*) and for "High Water" (*He made it to Kansas City, Twelfth Street and Vine* is literally copied), and the song from which radio maker Dylan says in 2006: "You all know this song, and it's always good" (*Theme Time Radio Hour* episode 20, "Musical Map").

Harrison himself edited "Let's Stick Together" in 1969 and turned it into "Let's Work Together", with the classic line *Together we will stand, divided we'll fall*. He scores a modest hit with it. But in 1970 it becomes for Canned Heat the biggest hit in the band's long career (number 2 in the UK, bigger than "On The Road Again" and "Going Up The Country"). However, both Ferry and Dylan prefer the less preachy, more pure rock variant "Let's Stick Together".

It is, after "Shenandoah", the second time that thematic or textual lines can be drawn from *Down In The Groove* to "Mississippi", providing yet again some insight into Dylan's working method and sources of inspiration, and illustrating Dylan's own wording of his working method:

> What happens is, I'll take a song I know and simply start playing it in my head. That's the way I meditate. A lot of people will look at a crack on the wall and meditate, or count sheep or angels or money or something, and it's a proven fact that it'll help them relax. I don't meditate on any of that stuff. I meditate on a song. I'll be playing Bob Nolan's *Tumbling Tumbleweeds*, for instance, in my head constantly — while I'm driving a car or talking to a person or sitting around or whatever. People will think they are talking to me and I'm talking back, but I'm not. I'm listening to the song in my head. At a certain point, some of the words will change and I'll start writing a song.

> (Robert Hilburn interview, 2003)

In the run up to "Mississippi" quite a few songs are *playing in the head*, apparently. And *Down In The Groove* reveals some of them. The *stick with me* from "Let's Stick Together"; the hopeless narrator in "Sally Sue Brown" is *goin' south* to humiliate himself in front of Sally Sue again; and the desolate state of the protagonist in "Mississippi" is an echo of what Dylan already heard from his beloved Stanley Brothers, in "Rank Strangers To Me":

I wandered again to my home in the mountains
Where in youth's early dawn I was happy and free
I looked for my friends but I never could find them
I found they were all rank strangers to me

Still, the apotheosis, the brille of the final line *things should start to get interesting right about now* does not come from a song that haunts Dylan, but is one of the three or four selfless contributions by soulmate Henry Rollins:

I shook 1992 by the neck
The road shot into me
Now there's only 1993
Don't attach
Hit hard
Disappear into the treeline
Keep moving
It gets harder to get up in the morning
Lines on my face
It should start getting interesting right about now
(Now Watch Him Die, 1993)

Rollins, the great, multitalented artist from Washington, District of Columbia, and in every conceivable respect the opposite of the distinguished Geordie Bryan Ferry from Washington, County Durham.

XIV Unca Donald

My clothes are wet, tight on my skin
Not as tight as the corner that I painted myself in
I know that fortune is waitin' to be kind
So give me your hand and say you'll be mine

Claustrophobic words indeed, the words with which the narrator describes his current state of mind. Surely, the most famous scene of some hero trapping himself in the corner while painting is Donald Duck, but there it is not oppressive. Donald locks himself in to avoid an obligatory "social" with Daisy, so as not to have to accompany her to one of those stupid social events where Daisy is always so eager to show up.

At first it is tempting to take the opening metaphor literally; wet clothes sticking to his skin... maybe he really did swim across that wide river to reach his beloved. But no - the second line, with the paint metaphor, suggests that the image of the wet, sticky clothes is a first step to yet another *accumulatio*, in this song the third accumulation of more or less similar images.

In terms of content we are back to the first *accumulatio*, in which the narrator also indicated to be "boxed in", "trapped", with "nowhere to escape". This quatrain provides the corresponding images: the anguish of the tight, sticky clothes, and like Donald, painted into the corner, *nowhere to escape.*

The coincidental resemblance with Duckburg's most famous resident will receive a remarkable psychological deepening in the next line. *Fortune waiting to be kind* are striking words to characterise the Donald Duck as it was created by Carl Barks. The brilliant Carl Barks, who managed to transcend the anonymity of "the good Duck artist", is the creator of Duckburg, the creator of Scrooge McDuck and Gladstone Gander, of Neighbor J. Jones and the Beagle Boys, in short: of the Donald Duck as etched in our collective memory. He is the man who turns the side-figure Donald, the impetuous, frantic pusher next to Mickey Mouse (in *The Wise Little Hen* and in *Orphan's Benefit*, 1934) into a protagonist with the image as we know him today: the Eternal Loser, the schmuck. Similar to Charlie Brown, for example, or Basil Fawlty - and to the narrator of "Mississippi".

They are usually popular heroes with the public. Perhaps even more popular than the underdog, who usually wins at the end of the film or story. Dramatists can explain that phenomenon: a bad ending "you take home with you", lets you lie awake at night. Shakespeare, Lessing, Brecht... that's why they like to write tragedies, plays in which the main character has to die - because the impact is many times greater than a happy ending. The original storytellers were aware of that too, by the way. At Perrault, Little Red Riding Hood is eaten, and finito. No fuss with some hunter cutting open the wolf's belly, and whatnot (*Le petit chaperon rouge*, 1697).

The less poignant variant of those fatal tragedies are the stories with the schmuck, who at least does survive his adventure. In Jewish humour and literature, the schmuck has existed as an archetype for centuries; in Western culture it has become increasingly popular since the second half of the twentieth century. Culminating in the 1990s, when Beck scores a mega hit with the schmuck's signature song "Loser", when The Big Lebowski becomes the new cult hero, when entire halls roar along with Radiohead's "Creep" and comedians like Louis C.K. and Seth Rogen lay the foundation for their success: the loser personage.

The most heart-breaking then are the losers like Donald Duck and Charlie Brown, the unlucky ones who so often have happiness at their fingertips. In the music it is most movingly portrayed by John Hiatt in the beautiful song "You May Already Be A Winner" (Riding With The King, 1983):

> *Dry your eyes pretty girl*
> *I just got news from the outside world*
> *I don't know how they got our names*
> *But yesterday this letter came*
> *"Mr. and Mrs. Resident Dweller, your lucky number is...*
> *You may already be a winner!"*
>
> *Well, I've suspected this for years*
> *Still in all its good to hear*
> *They're pulling for us in the post*
> *To you my dear, I raise this toast*

But the most beautiful words for exactly this state of mind are of course chosen by the Nobel laureate: "*I know that fortune is waiting to be kind*".

Variants of the one-liner can be found in Dylan's record cabinet. With Charlie Daniels for instance, on his rather obscure, nameless debut album from 1970, which he is allowed to record after he assisted Dylan on *Nashville Skyline* and on *Self Portrait*. It is a remarkably rugged, kaleidoscopic country rock album by an untamed, extremely talented ruffian (highlight is the closing "Thirty Nine Miles From Mobile", a hard rocking, Allman Brothers-like jam), with halfway through the beautiful "Georgia", which sounds like a left-over from *Music From The Big Pink*. In which Charlie sings:

> All of my life I've been told
> That the LA streets was paved with gold
> Fame and fortune waiting to reward ya
> But it didn't take long to understand
> California ain't the promised land
> But at least a man's a man in Georgia

A more improbable, but equally striking source is an English Puritan Baptist preacher from the nineteenth century, the "prince of preachers" Charles Haddon Spurgeon, a prolific author of Christian books, hymns and sermons still popular in Calvinist circles today. In 1866 he collects all psalms and Christian hymns in *Our Own Hymn Book*, and number 499 therein, attributed to one Hewett, is "Seek And Ye Shall Find":

> Come, poor sinner, come and see,
> All thy strength is found in me;
> I am waiting to be kind,
> To relieve thy troubled mind.

Still, Dylan does use the most unlikely sources. More attractive, however, is a source like Charlie Daniels. Or the so admired Bing Crosby ("quite a man, quite a singer," as Dylan says in *Theme Time Radio Hour*), whose charming "Meet The Sun Half-Way" also has such a similar "fortune waiting to be kind"-oneliner:

> *Stop hiding behind a pillow whenever the dawn looks gray,*
> *Get up, get out, and meet the sun half-way!*
> *There may be a fortune waiting, or maybe an egg souffle,*
> *Get out, get out, and meet the sun half-way!*

And this Bing Crosby song becomes even more attractive when the last verse is sung:

> *You may be a new Dick Tracy, conducting an exposé*
> *Get up, get out, and meet the sun half-way!*
> *Now don't you blame your luck, say, do you want to sound like Donald Duck?*
> *You know, when you smile, you throw yourself a big bouquet!*

But then again, Donald Duck would, obviously, have swam to the other side of that wide river without any problems.

And finally, the sweet closing line *So give me your hand and say you'll be mine* completes the eclectic character of this exceptional quatrain.

Jesus has a small supporting role in Monty Python's *Life Of Brian* (1979). We see him in the scene "Jesus' Lack of Crowd Control", the scene in which Brian and his mother, on their way to the stoning, do happen to pass by Jesus, just starting his "Sermon on the Mount".

It is hardly a spectacular performance. Jesus speaks insecurely and too soft, the audience is noisy and easily distracted. "Mr. Cheeky" (Eric Idle) can't stay focused either, and finds it more entertaining to harass the nose picking "Mr. Big Nose".

> MAN #2: You hear that? Blessed are the Greek.
> GREGORY: The Greek?
> MAN #2: Mmm. Well, apparently, he's going to inherit the earth.
> GREGORY: Did anyone catch his name?
> MRS. BIG NOSE: You're not going to thump anybody.
> MR. BIG NOSE: I'll thump him if he calls me 'Big Nose' again.
> MR. CHEEKY: Oh, shut up, Big Nose.
> MR. BIG NOSE: Ah! All right. I warned you. I really will slug you so hard--
> MRS. BIG NOSE: Oh, it's the meek! Blessed are the meek! Oh, that's nice, isn't it? I'm glad they're getting something, 'cause they have a hell of a time.

The poor, pathetically awkward Jesus is played by Kenneth Coley, who can be admired in these same months in the BBC production *Measure For Measure*, the television adaptation of Shakespeare's play. Coley will have seen the link with the "Sermon on the Mount" when rehearsing his text for *Life Of Brian*: *For with what judgment ye judge, ye shall be judged: and with what measure ye mete, it shall be measured to you again* (Matt. 7:2).

Kenneth Coley is standing at the same crossroads of Shakespeare and the Bible that will inspire Dylan more than once. "The Sermon on the Mount" provides references and idiom for songs like "Up To Me", "Buckets Of Rain", "Angelina", "Mr. Tambourine Man" and "The Groom's Still Waiting At The Altar", and delivers in these same days of *Life Of Brian* and BBC's *Measure For Measure* jargon and theme for "Do Right To Me Baby" (*don't wanna judge nobody, don't wanna be judged*).

Dylan used *Measure For Measure*'s plot a long time ago for "Seven Curses" (1963), although the format for this particular song probably is the old folksong "Anathea". Presumably, 21-year-old Dylan is not yet that familiar with Shakespeare's use of the same storyline - the plot around the dirty old judge who falsely promises a fair maiden to save her lover from the gallows in exchange for sex.

The young bard soon fills the knowledge gap. Shakespeare and his oeuvre still get only superficial name checks in "Highway 61 Revisited", "Desolation Row" and "Stuck Inside Of Mobile", but from *The Basement Tapes* (1967) Dylan processes longer quotes and paraphrases with more substantive relevance for the lyrics in question. "Tears Of Rage", of course, and "Too Much Of Nothing" in particular, and Professor Christopher Ricks ultimately finds a total of forty references in Dylan's oeuvre - although it should be noted: sometimes *very* far-fetched.

Not too far-fetched, though, is this one appropriation in "Mississippi", literally lifted from *Measure For Measure*:

DUKE VINCENTIO
If he be like your brother, for his sake
Is he pardon'd; and, for your lovely sake,
Give me your hand and say you will be mine.

From the last act, in the BBC adaptation faithfully, verbatim spoken by Kenneth Coley, who in 1979 is the physical manifestation of the Dylan Crossroads, somewhere in Mississippi; the crossing of Shakespeare Alley and Sermon Mountain Row.

XV   Gaze into the abyss

Well, the emptiness is endless, cold as the clay
You can always come back, but you can't come back all the way
Only one thing I did wrong
Stayed in Mississippi a day too long

 Friedrich Nietzsche most certainly has a thing for music. As early as 1858, at the age of fourteen, many years before declaring God dead, he calls music "this most glorious gift of God my companion on my life's journey", and states in the same article ("On Music"):

> God gave us music so that we, first and foremost, will be guided upward by it. All qualities are united in music: it can lift us up, it can be capricious, it can cheer us up and delight us, nay, with its soft, melancholy tunes, it can even break the resistance of the toughest character.

He remains faithful to music throughout his life, studying music theory and piano with zeal, writing some seventy classical compositions (mostly for piano), and even playing with the idea of becoming a professional composer -

but both Wagner and Hans von Bülow advise against it. He's just not talented enough. Von Bülow's rejection, after Nietzsche sent him his "Manfred-Meditation", has an entertaining, Nietzschean cruelty, by the way:

> I could not discover in it the least trace of Apollonian elements, and, as for the Dionysian, to tell you frankly, it made me think of the morning after a bacchanalian orgy rather than of an orgy itself.... Once again — don't take this too badly — you yourself say your music is "detestable" — it is, actually, more detestable than you believe.

And a little further on Von Bülow even calls the piece "the most unedifying and anti-musical instance of notes placed on music paper that I have come across in a long time" and a "rape of Euterpe", a rape of the muse of flute playing and lyrical poetry.

Well, that might be a little too rich. Nietzsche's music really isn't *that* awful. "A gifted amateur" is the friendlier, and a better qualification. And with the miraculous, enchanting "Das Fragment an sich" (*The fragment by itself,* 1871) Nietzsche actually writes, twenty years before Satie, the first piece of minimal music in music history. Moreover, in 1896 his philosophical and literary work inspires Richard Strauss to write the overwhelming symphonic poem "Also sprach Zarathustra" (which will become the soundtrack to the endless emptiness in *2001: A Space Odyssey*). And Nietzsche's work inspires Gustav Mahler to write music to "O Mensch! Gib Acht!" (*O man! Take heed!*) from his greatest work, the Third Symphony; hardly insignificant contributions to classical music, all in all.

An important part of his modest oeuvre consists of songs. And although Nietzsche certainly is a great poet, he prefers to set other people's poems to music - which often have similarities with Nietzsche's thinking and works. Like "Aus der Jugendzeit" (*From the times of youth*), by Friedrich Rückert, in which *emptiness* is the theme, the emptiness one experiences upon the realisation: *you can't go back all the way*:

> *Once the heart is emptied, the heart is emptied,*
> *it never becomes full again.*

The French phenomenon Jules Michelet (1798-1874), who like Dylan in his later work tries to recreate the past, is touched by Rückert's poem and incorporates parts of it in his poem "L'Hirondelle" (*The Swallow*, 1861):

> *Mais le vide du coeur reste, mais reste le vide du coeur,*
> *Et rien ne le remplira*
> *(But the heart's emptiness remains; its emptiness remains,*
> *And nothing will make it full again)*

... which again is picked up by Vincent Van Gogh, who quotes it when he tries to express in his letters to brother Theo how much and why he is touched by the *endless emptiness*. This one example is from the letter to Theo of 10 April 1882, but *emptiness* and *endlessness* is an inexhaustible source of inspiration for Vincent throughout his creative life, as well as an image of doom, as can be seen with increasing frequency from the letters just before his end:

> I can't precisely describe what the thing I have is like, there
> are terrible fits of anxiety sometimes – without any
> apparent cause – or then again a feeling of emptiness and
> fatigue in the mind.

Vincent writes this to his sister Willemien a year before his death. Thematically similar to one of his last letters, two weeks before his suicide:

> Knowing clearly what I wanted I've painted another three large canvases since then. They're immense stretches of wheatfields under angry skies, and I made a point of trying to express despondency, extreme loneliness.

It is of all times, the fascination for the Void, the endless emptiness and the Nothing. The Nothing has occupied philosophers since Democritus, twenty-five centuries ago, most religions begin The Creation with a Nothing from which a world is created and it inspires artists like Ovid; Homer; Dante, Blake with his obsession for "the abominable void", "the endless abyss of space and the curtains of darkness round the Void"; it inspires Baudelaire staring from his balcony into the *espace profond*, into the deep void; Rimbaud, whose *Season in Hell* is a "fall into the void"; and Kerouac, who tries to ward off the void on almost every page of *Desolation Angels*.
But closest to the poet Dylan is, of course, Allen Ginsberg:

> *not even the human*
> *imagination satisfies*
> *the endless emptiness*
> *of the soul*
> ("Over Kansas", 1954)

For this last "Mississippi" quatrain, Dylan only borrows that image of the *endless emptiness*, without further thematizing it - just like the following *cold as clay* is an atmospheric and melodic, but hardly eloquent cliché. They too are fragments that, as Dylan says in that *New York Times* interview, "write themselves", floating around somewhere in that *stream-of-consciousness* and now surfacing.

The word combination *cold* and *clay* then probably entered Dylan's vocabulary via "Tom Dooley", a long, long time ago:

> *I dug a grave four feet long, I dug it three feet deep,*
> *Throwed cold clay o'er her, and tromped it with my feet.*

"Tom Dooley" is the Kingston Trio's biggest hit in 1958 (estimated sales between four and six million singles), and, according to music historians and specialists like John Fogerty and Joan Baez, is the spark that ignited the folk revival. The song is an arrangement of a nineteenth-century folk song about the Southern soldier Thomas C. Dula, hung in 1868 after the murder of his fiancée Laura Foster. The impact of that story on him, or at least the impact of the song, Dylan does not hide; as early as 1965 he mentions Dooley in the liner notes of Highway 61 Revisited:

> when tom dooley, the kind of person you think you've seen before, comes strolling in with White Heap, the hundred Inevitables all say "who's that man who looks so white?"

In 2020 the old murder ballad is apparently still floating around in that stream-of-consciousness: *Take me to the place Tom Dooley was hung*, says Dylan in "Murder Most Foul". And he's not the only one who is struck by Tom Dooley and that *cold clay*. Elvis Costello borrows the image for two songs, as he tells in his autobiography *Unfaithful Music & Disappearing Ink*:

"I could point you to lines in my songs that use the language of folk songs: from the allusion to *Barbara Allen* in *I Want You* to the cold clay pulled out of Doc Watson's rendition of *Tom Dooley*, which turns up in *Suit of Lights* and then again in *Tramp the Dirt Down*.

The poet Dylan's grandeur shines in the sequel, setting those half-known images of despair into the crown borrowed from Henry Rollins: *You can always come back, but you can't come back all the way.* After all, the emptiness remains - an emptied heart never fills up again.

Or, as Nietzsche would say: if you gaze too long into the abyss, the abyss will gaze back into you.

XVI The piano pounding madman

 In 1979 Jerry Lee Lewis records a dazzling, steamy cover of Dylan's throwaway from the *Desire* sessions (1976), "Rita May", the only noteworthy cover of that particular song anyone has managed.

Lewis, according to legend, demonstrates his unworldliness afterwards, when he has asked producer Bones Howe who wrote that song. "Bob Dylan," Howe answers with a broad grin, for he is sure Lewis will be mighty surprised. But Lewis shows no recognition at all. "That boy is good," says Jerry Lee Lewis, "I'll do anything by him."

"Anything" might be a bit of an exaggeration, but indeed: thirty-five years later, in 2014, Dylan producer Daniel Lanois will collaborate on *Rock & Roll Time* of the then 79-year-old rock 'n' legend. Lanois points to the existence of another forgotten little ditty, of "Stepchild" from 1978. Jerry Lee takes the bait and repeats his '79 feat: the cover is undeniably the most exciting version of "Stepchild"; unwieldy, swampy and irresistible. Whether he by now knows who Dylan is, the historiography does not mention.

Conversely, there is a self-evident admiration. Most explicitly expressed in *Theme Time Radio Hour*, where radio maker Dylan finds, no fewer than seven times, an excuse to play a record by The Killer. Usually introduced with extensive information about "the piano pounding madman", his tumultuous youth, his dubious predilection for young girls and its consequences, and remarkable facts from his career - such as Lewis' role as Iago in *Catch My Soul*, the 1968 rock musical adaptation of *Othello*, which allows Dylan to play "Lust of the Blood" in episode 81, *Blood*:

> Ya know if anyone ever asks me why I do this radio show I can just play 'em that. Jerry Lee Lewis singing Shakespeare -- that's what this show is all about.

Episode 31 has the theme *Tennessee,* so Jerry Lee is unavoidable, as the DJ says ("You can't stop off in Tennessee without paying a visit to the Killer.") Dylan chooses "Night Train to Memphis", and thus passes The Killer's other ode to Memphis, "Memphis Beat" from 1966. Not out of ignorance; we know for sure that Dylan has the LP of the same name in his record cabinet.

Memphis Beat, like many other records of the piano beast, is a compilation of Jerry Lee's compositions, songs written especially for Lewis, and covers. Half of the songs were recorded at the Phillips Studio in Memphis in January '66, other songs have been waiting eight months to be released and were recorded in New York and the album contains even two songs from a recording session in 1963. In all, less than half an hour, but it is still a reasonably successful album. The opener

"Memphis Beat", is an attractive run-of-the-mill smasher, written for Jerry Lee by two members of the *Nashville Songwriters Hall of Fame*, Allen Reynolds and Dickey Lee. The lyrics seem to come straight from the Memphis Tourist Office brochure:

> *Well they got people a-walkin'*
> *And ridin' and swimmin'*
> *Just tryin' to get a chance at them good lookin' women*
> *Now we just march on down to the foot of Beale Street*
> *Ah then dance all night to that Memphis Beat*

Anyway, songwriter Dickey Lee is no small fry, of course. On this same album is Jerry's cover of Dickey Lee's biggest hit, the immortal, "She Thinks I Still Care". Recorded by Elvis, Johnny Cash, The Flying Burrito Brothers, Gene Pitney, John Fogerty, James Taylor and others – after acquiring its monument status through Dylan's idol George Jones (1962), the country god of whom Dylan says:

> Looking through my record collection the other day, I've got about 70 George Jones albums. If you look at 'em all, it gives you a great history of men's haircuts.

In between are some more and less successful renditions of songs like Jimmy Reed's "Big Boss Man" and Stick McGhee's smoothly swinging "Drinkin' Wine Spo-Dee-O-Dee", with which he will score another small hit. Downright awkward is the tear-jerking doo-wop "Too Young" ("They're trying to tell us we're too young"). Awkward not only because of the corny lounge arrangement, but especially because of the lyrics, sung by the man who torpedoed his own career by marrying his thirteen-year-old niece Myra.

Most curious, however, is the only self-written song on the LP, "Lincoln Limousine".

"Lincoln Limousine" is Jerry Lee's bizarre ode to Kennedy. According to biographer Joe Bonomo in the great biography *Jerry Lee Lewis: Lost And Found* (2009) "one the most peculiar tracks he's cut in his career" and

> Jerry Lee's odd tribute to John F. Kennedy is simply weird, so ambiguous and amateurishly written that it's impossible to determine exactly what motivated him to write it.

The biographer does have a point. What to think of verses like:

> *Well they shot him in the back seat of a Lincoln limousine*
> *Was a great, great leader by the name of Kennedy*
> *He fought for right and freedom, tried to keep this nation clean*
> *But they shot him in the backseat of a Lincoln limousine*
>
> *And he had ten million dollars, had the world right in his hand*
> *But a twenty dollar rifle cut the life of this great man*
> *He had a lovely wife and two children seldom seen*
> *But they shot him in the backseat of a Lincoln limousine*

So clumsy it almost seems deliberate, indeed. Miles away from The Byrds' "He Was A Friend Of Mine", Kris Kristofferson's "They Killed Him" or Dion's "Abraham, Martin And John", in any case.

It could not have inspired Dylan to his "Kennedy song" "Murder Most Foul" (2020) either, but "Lincoln Limousine" does have some impact: the intro, the first ten notes, Dylan copies almost one-on-one for the final "Mississippi" version, the *"Love And Theft"* version - the only studio version with this intro, by the way. The same lick is used as a bridge and the bard is very content with it, apparently: in the live performances of 2001 he plays the intro twice, in later performances the lick will be integrated in even more places in the song (as with Mark Knopfler in Zurich, 2011). But just as often he skips it, unfortunately.

In any case: at least once one little melody by Jerry Lee Lewis, despite all his qualities not a great songwriter, penetrates Dylan's oeuvre. "He sings this song, he pounds the piano. He says he wrote it and that's good enough for me," as the radio producer says in one of his last *Theme Time Radio Hours*, "Clearance Sale", April 2009.

The song "Memphis Beat" gets a second life in the twenty-first century. Television company TNT produces the comic police series *Memphis Beat* in 2010 and blues musician and five-time Grammy Award winner Keb' Mo' is asked for the soundtrack. He has Jerry Lee Lewis on a pedestal and records a very nice cover of the song for the opening theme. The show is not a big success (after two seasons the plug is pulled again), but songwriter Dickey Lee can't complain. "She Still Thinks I Care" is of course his goose with golden eggs, but:

> There are still seven or eight songs that have paid off consistently. I can't believe it, but it's still mailbox money.
> (interview *Nashville Music Guide,* February 14, 2012)

XVII Between Point Dume and Oxnard

It's a long, laborious delivery, the final version of "Mississippi", the wonderful version on *"Love & Theft"*. First recording attempts date from September '96 (Oxnard, California). In January '97 Dylan is in Miami with Lanois for the recording of *Time Out Of Mind*, with the well-known falling-out and subsequent discard of the song. And finally, the song is put to tape to the satisfaction of the master in May 2001.

We owe that final recording to, as Dylan reveals during the press conference July 2001 in Rome, the fortunate circumstance that those earlier recordings have not been leaked in the meantime, have not been distributed by bootleggers. When that happens, the song is *contaminated for me*, and Dylan won't look back;

> But, thank God, it never got out, so we recorded it again. But something like that would never have happened 10 years ago. You'd have probably all heard the trashy version of it and I'd have never re-recorded it.

Still, the "trashy version" may well serve to extract a few extra pennies from the fans' pockets seven years after that press conference; on *The Bootleg Series Vol 8: Tell Tale Signs* (2008) are three of those rejected versions from '96 and '97. All of them beautiful versions, certainly worth the money, and yet another demonstration of Dylan's incomprehensible take on his own songs. Dylan does have an opinion about that stubborn image too, in this same press meeting:

> I've been asked: 'So how come you're such a bad judge of your material?' I've been criticized for not putting my best songs on certain albums, but it is because I consider that the song isn't ready yet. It's not been recorded right.

Art history teaches us that this is not a very strong argument. Nabokov seems to have been on his way to the incinerator with *Lolita*'s manuscript (but was stopped by his wife). Claude Monet himself destroyed fifteen of his water lily paintings. Michelangelo had worked his brilliant *Pietà* for eight years and suddenly did not like it anymore; one leg of Christ had already been smashed to smithereens before a church official could intervene (the one-legged *Deposition* can still be admired in the Museo dell'Opera del Duomo in Florence).

Kafka was extremely reluctant to publish throughout his life, and at the unrelenting insistence of admiring friends only released a fraction. On his deathbed in the sanatorium, he begged his friend Max Brod to burn everything in his study at home – being most of Kafka's oeuvre, including masterpieces such as *Der Prozeß* and dozens of stories (Brod ignored the dying man's wish and published everything).

How it is possible that the artists are such bad critics of their own work, the question that Dylan tries to undo in that press conference, is not answered. Neither by Dylan, who in fact only repeats the question as he "answers" that the works are "not ready yet" or "not recorded right". A more persistent journalist would have asked; *what* does "Farewell Angelina" still miss, *what* exactly is wrong with the recording of "Blind Willie McTell"?

Though presumably the more persistent journalist had not received a satisfactory answer to this either. Not surprisingly, of course – it really *is* an impossible question, similar to "why do you like this song?". In Dylan's case, the dissatisfaction must have to do with the *sound*, the often elusive "colour" of a recording, a quality Dylan appreciates above all else, the quality he values higher than "the right words" or the beauty of a melody.

The story of engineer Mark Howard, both at *Time Out Of Mind* and *"Love And Theft"* the studio technician on duty, does illustrate this point quite well:

> Dylan was living in Point Dume, and he'd drive up every day, and he'd tune into this radio station that he could only get between Point Dume and Oxnard. It would just pop up at one point, and it was all these old blues recordings, Little Walter, guys like that. And he'd ask us, "Why do those records sound so great? Why can't anybody have a record sound like that anymore? Can I have that?" And so, I say, "Yeah, you can get those sound still." "Well," he says, "that's the sound I'm thinking of for this record.

But apparently, in 1996, in California, he couldn't get hold of that particular sound for "Mississippi" after all.

According to legend, we owe the final recording and release of "Mississippi" to a tenacious *Max Brod 2.0*: manager Jeff Rosen is a passionate fan of the song and is believed to have reminded Dylan after the recordings for *"Love And Theft"*. Which can in any case be deduced from the interview with drummer David Kemper, in the same beautiful *Tell Tale Signs Special* in *Uncut*, 2008:

> I know of two versions of "Mississippi". We thought we were done with *Love And Theft*, and then a friend of Bob's passed him a note, and he said, oh, yeah, I forgot about this: "Mississippi". And then he made a comment, did you guys ever bring the version we did down at the Lanois sessions. And they said, yeah, we have it right here. And he said let's listen to it. So they put it up on the big speakers, and I said, damn – release it!

Kemper is a fan, that much is clear. And is touched by the beauty of the song, the richness of the melodies and the grandeur of the lyrics - but, just like any other fan, is not receptive to what Dylan lacks; the "colour" or the *sound*.

Still, the melodic richness definitely is a distinguishing quality of the song. In general Dylan doesn't attach much importance to this - likewise on this album, most songs have only two or three chords, Dylan opting for simple blues schemes with a cast-iron lick and few adventurous variations. No problem, of course; after all, *in der Beschränkung zeigt sich der Meister*, as Goethe teaches, "It is in working within limits that the master reveals himself" and that Dylan can produce masterpieces within these limits he has already demonstrated dozens of times ("All Along The Watchtower", "Knockin' On Heaven's Door", "Desolation Row").

But every now and then a song pushes him to musically more challenging regions. "She's Your Lover Now" stumbles over his own melodic richness, "New Morning" is such a multi-coloured example and so is this "Mississippi".

The tireless Dylanwatcher and researcher Eyolf Østrem from Scandinavia, administrator of the beautiful blog *Things Twice* and compiler of the legendary "Neanderthal site" (his words) *dylanchords*, points to a second peculiarity: "Mississippi" is one of the very few Dylan songs with an ascending bass line:

```
G          /a     /b              /c
Got nothing for you, I had nothing before
/d              /e          F        G
Don't even have anything for myself anymore
G          /a  /b              /c
Sky full of fire, pain pouring down
/d              /e          F        G
Nothing you can sell me, I'll see you around.
```

... indeed, an ascending line that neatly climbs the whole scale alphabetically. "Like A Rolling Stone" does that too, but there aren't many other examples in Dylan's oeuvre. And there aren't too many outside of Dylan's oeuvre either. The chorus of The Eagles' first hit, "Take It Easy" (1972, written by Jackson Brown and Glenn Frey) has partly the same scheme (under *"Don't let the sound of your own wheels drive you crazy"*), but that's about it.

Like "Blind Willie McTell" and "Make You Feel My Love", the cover is released before the original. After Dylan rejected the song for *Time Out Of Mind*, he donated it to Sheryl Crow, who records it for her album *The Globe Sessions* (1998). That version may have inspired Dylan to give it another shot himself; Crows "Mississippi" is okay but lacks *shine*, with a rather joyless and awkward *Whoo!* finishing it off.

The Dixie Chicks fare a lot better, with a dazzling and sparkling interpretation on the live album *Top Of The World Tour* (2003). Same approach as Crow, but with real pleasure, passion and thrust (bursting from every single live performance). A small lyrical adjustment does reveal that all the ladies are a bit less tough than the image they are trying to maintain, though:

> I was thinkin' 'bout the things that **you** said
> I was dreaming I was sleepin' in **your** bed

...apparently a possible homoerotic suspicion is a little too scary for both Sheryl Crow and The Chicks' powerhouse Natalie Maines, so they'd rather turn the sung *Rosie* into a gender-neutral *you*. Musically, The Chicks more than compensate for the slip. The organ part from The Who's "Won't Get Fooled Again" in the *split to splinters*-couplet, for instance, is a golden find.

In June 2020 The Dixie Chicks will also change their own name, for politically correct reasons, to The Chicks, *to meet this moment*, as the official statement says. In 2003 Maines had declared from the podium that she was ashamed of President Bush and the Iraq war, which led to a long, hefty hate campaign including death threats. Since then, The Chicks have been more sensitive to *the right thing to do*. Fortunately, "Mississippi" isn't "wrong" yet; in 2020 the song is still on the setlist.

Remarkably, the best version so far comes from Scotland. Veteran Rab Noakes plays live a sober, compelling version in which he manages to bring together both the folky Dylan from 1961 and the elderly troubadour from 2001. Just an acoustic Gibson and Noakes' relaxed, light-hearted, somewhat hoarse rendition... proving you *can* come back all the way, after all.

Sing in me, o Muse

So what does it all mean? Myself and a lot of other songwriters have been influenced by these very same themes. And they can mean a lot of different things. If a song moves you, that's all that's important. I don't have to know what a song means. I've written all kinds of things into my songs. And I'm not going to worry about it – what it all means. [...] I don't know what it means, either. But it sounds good. And you want your songs to sound good.

- Dylan, *The Nobel Lecture,* 2017

Most of the chapters of this book have been published previously as articles on the English site *Untold Dylan,* June-July 2020

From the same author in English:

- *Blonde On Blonde.*
Bob Dylan's mercurial masterpiece, 2016

- *Blood On The Tracks.*
Dylan's masterpiece in blue, 2018

- *The Basement Tapes*
Bob Dylan's summer of 1967, 2020

- *Desolation Row*
Bob Dylan's poetic letter from 1965, 2020

- *Where Are You Tonight (Journey Through Dark Heat)*
Bob Dylan's hushed-up classic from 1978, 2020

Thanks

Tom Willems, from *bobdylaninnederland.blogspot.nl* - the mercury Dylan blog

Martin Bierens - dear old Bobhead in Ireland, from Utrecht to Amsterdam in Holland to Dornbirn in Austria to Stadskanaal to Tilburg to Bielefeld in Germany

Tony Attwood in England - webmaster of *Untold Dylan,* the place where it's always safe and warm

The author

Bob Dylan's songs continue to fascinate.

Jochen Markhorst (1964) grew up in Arnhem, The Netherlands and in Hanover, Germany, with *Highway 61 Revisited* and *Blonde On Blonde* as soundtrack, bought *Blood On The Tracks* and *Street Legal* from his pocket money, studied German language at Utrecht University, translated Russian at the Military Intelligence Service, teaches language training courses at companies and lessons in schools, translates German literature, Dutch websites and English subtitles and always the music of Dylan is playing in the background.

Markhorst, however, is not one of the hardliners who honour the motto *Nobody Sings Dylan Like Dylan* – Jimi Hendrix is certainly not the only one who can brush up a Dylan song. He preaches this controversial opinion, among other things, in his ten books on Dylan songs, and continues to build on the Dylan library.

Jochen has been living in Utrecht for the past 37 years, is still married to the same great, attractive woman and has two sons who have left home by now, but fortunately still work and live in Utrecht.

Printed in Great Britain
by Amazon